The LEMON Cookbook

by
Eleanor Freemark

Illustrations by
Michelle Burchard

HPBooks
a division of
PRICE STERN SLOAN
Los Angeles

Cover photo by Burke/Triolo Photography

Published by HPBooks
a division of Price Stern Sloan, Inc.
11150 Olympic Boulevard
Los Angeles, California 90064
©1993 Eleanor Freemark
Cover photo and illustrations ©1993 Price Stern Sloan, Inc.

Library of Congress Cataloging-in-Publication Data

Freemark, Eleanor
  The lemon cookbook / by Eleanor Freemark.
      p.   cm.
  Includes index.
  ISBN 1-55788-061-1
  1. Cookery (Lemons)   I. Title.
TX813.L4F74   1993
641.6'4334—dc20   92-44770
  CIP

Printed in the United States of America

10 9 8 7 6 5 4 3 2 1

NOTICE: The information in this book is true and complete to the best of our knowledge. All recommendations are made without any guarantees on the part of the author or Price Stern Sloan. The author and publisher disclaim all liability in connection with the use of this information.

This book is printed on acid-free paper.

Acknowledgments

I wish to acknowledge my husband, Larry, for his love and encouragement, and continued support, and for his addiction to lemons which first inspired this book. I also wish to thank my daughter, Liz, for some of the recipes in this book, including the great Lemon Ice Cream, and my friend, Jeanne, for her help in putting the manuscript together, and all my other family and friends for forsaking their diets to taste and test these recipes.

About This Book

This book was inspired by my husband, who is a lemon lover of the highest degree. It is dedicated to him and to all of those who love the tart, intense flavor of lemons. It is also dedicated to those who prefer just a subtle hint of lemon, like myself. Knowing that there are all kinds of "politically correct lemon lovers," the amounts of lemon juice and peel called for in these recipes are designed to encompass us all. Although the recipes range from very simple to fairly complex, they are all easy to prepare and the ingredients are widely available.

I remember watching a great New York chef being interviewed on a TV talk show many years ago. He was very, very portly. He said he never ate a meal; the only way to cook was to taste, taste and retaste, and he tasted all day long. I was very impressed and have seriously taken his long-ago advice, to taste, especially when preparing something new. I encourage you to do the same.

Cooking is not only for professionals. Recipes in cookbooks need not be followed as if they were written in stone, even those recipes by the greatest of chefs. Each of us has different tastes, and ingredients vary as to freshness, texture and flavor. We can all be creative—even the beginning cook. That's what makes cooking fun.

Use this book as a guide. Taste right from the beginning. Adjust ingredients such as herbs, spices, onions, garlic, oils, creams and sugar to your own and your family's individual tastes. Adjust yogurt, milk, cottage cheese and other dairy products to taste. Also try substituting lowfat or nonfat products to cut calories and cholesterol. You will spot many instances where you can do your own thing. Cooking is both serious and light-hearted. The rewards are immediate. Have fun with this book!

Contents

All about Lemons

The lemon is a tree-borne citrus fruit, closely related to the orange. Lemons originated in India, and were brought to Europe by Arab traders during the twelfth century. Lemons are grown extensively in Italy, Spain, Cyprus and Israel, as well as California, Arizona and Florida.

The lemon tree bears fruit every day of the year. A lemon tree becomes fully productive around the tenth year of life. A single tree can yield approximately 1500 lemons, although some trees have been known to yield twice that amount.

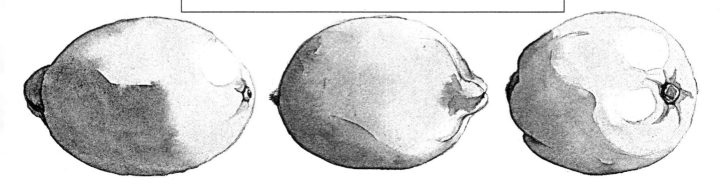

Buying & Storing Lemons

- Buy lemons with a rich yellow color, a thin smooth-textured skin and a slight shine. To measure juiciness, lemons should be heavy for their size and feel firm. (A paler color usually means a very fresh lemon with a higher acidity level.)

- Do not buy lemons that are dark yellow, or that have a dull skin, a hardened skin, a shriveled skin, soft green spots or small pricks in the skin.

- Wash lemons thoroughly in soapy water, then rinse to remove any chemical spray.

- If lemons are to be used within a week, they need not be refrigerated. Add fragrance and decoration to your kitchen by placing lemons in a pretty bowl on your kitchen counter top.

- Refrigerated lemons will last a month stored in a vegetable crisper or plastic bag.

- Lemons can be frozen for up to 12 months. They can be peeled, sectioned and dry-packed or frozen with a bit of their own juice. Lemons can also be packed in a syrup made with lemon juice and honey and sealed in freezer bags. If sections are frozen with juice, allow room for expansion.

Special Utensils for Lemons

- Small, sharp stainless steel knife for cutting lemons

- Small juicer for squeezing one or two lemons (For squeezing larger amounts, use a small electric juicer.)

- Small grater for grating lemon peel

- Zester for removing peel in very fine strips

- Citrus peeler for removing lemon peel in long wide strips

- Magic peeler for scoring lemons, making it easy to remove peel in quarters

Tips for Working with Lemons

- Lemons give juice more easily at room temperature. If the lemons are refrigerated, bring them to room temperature by placing in a microwave oven 20 seconds on MEDIUM power, or roll lemons firmly between palms of your hands or on a hard surface to break open the little juice sacs.

- For grating lemon peel, a zester is easier on your hands than a grater. However, if a zester is used, the thin strips of peel should be very finely chopped with a sharp knife or grated in a small electric grinder.

- When peeling, do not remove any part of the white pith, as it is very bitter.

- Grate peel over waxed paper before cutting lemon.

- Wrap grated peel in a plastic bag when preparing it in advance. (Air dries out lemon peel.) Store in refrigerator or freezer.

- Lemons that have been peeled must be stored in plastic bags and used within 3 days.

- Avoid using aluminum pots when cooking with lemons. (The acids in lemon leach aluminum.)

Lemon Equivalents

- 1 medium-size lemon yields 2 to 3 tablespoons of juice

- 1 large lemon yields 3 to 4 tablespoons of juice

- 1 medium to large lemon yields 1 tablespoon of grated peel

- 4 to 6 lemons yield 1 cup (8 oz.) of juice

Lemon Garnishes

Lemon Cups

Great for serving a variety of party dips, lemon sauces, ice creams and ices. Cut lemon in half, crosswise. (Juice lemon with a fork and store juice for future use.) Using a curved grapefruit knife, cut out lemon flesh and carefully scrape remainder of flesh and as much of the white inner skin (pith) as possible. Freeze in plastic bags until ready to use.

Lemon Slices & Lemon Wedges

Serve with fish, salads, hors d'oeuvres and drinks. To make lemon slices, cut off both ends of the lemon. Slice center of lemon into rounds 1/8 to 1/4 inch thick. Serve as whole slices or cut slices in halves or quarters. To make lemon wedges, cut lengthwise 6 to 8 equal sections with a sharp knife. If desired, sections can be marked with a citrus peeler before slicing.

Lemon Halves

Serve with fish. Cut each lemon in half. Wrap lemon halves in 6-inch rounds of cheese cloth and twist edges together and seal. (Lemon wraps can be purchased at fish markets or specialty food stores.)

Lemon Twists

Serve with drinks or float in punch bowls. Cut lemon slice from one edge to center of slice. Core center. Twist cut sides in opposite directions. (When placing lemon slices on drink glasses, do not twist.)

Lemon Peel Twist

Use for decorating individual plates, platters or drinks. Using a citrus peeler, start at one end of lemon. Cut lemon peel around the lemon. Cut peel into 2-inch strips. Curl peel and twist in opposite directions.

NUTRITIONAL INFORMATION ON LEMONS

Serving size: 1 lemon

27 Calories
90.1 g Water
1.1 g Protein
0.3 g Fat
8.2 g Carbohydrate
0.4 g Fiber
26 mg Calcium
16 mg Phosphorus

0.6 mg Iron
2 mg Sodium
138 mg Potassium
20 I.U. Vitamin A
0.04 mg Thiamin
0.02 mg Riboflavin
0.1 mg Niacin
53 mg Vitamin C

High in Vitamin C: 1 tablespoon (15 g) of fresh lemon juice provides a 11 percent of the Recommended Daily Allowance of Vitamin C; 1 (2-1/2-inch diameter) medium-size lemon provides 63 percent of the Recommended Daily Allowance of Vitamin C.

Appetizers & Sandwiches

Appetizers, whether served as finger foods or arranged more formally for a sit-down dinner, are the perfect opener for a festive meal or party. The recipes included in this chapter have just the right hint of lemon to add interest to the   beginning of your meal.

Fruit Platter

Fruit serves as an alternative to vegetable hors d'oeuvres.

1/2 fresh pineapple, cut into chunks, or 1 cup
   canned pineapple chunks
1 cup melon balls (cantaloupe, honeydew,
   Crenshaw or Persian melon)
1 cup strawberries, with stems
1 red apple, unpeeled, quartered
1 pear, unpeeled, quartered
Sesame-Lemon Dressing (page 29)
Mint sprigs
Maraschino cherries

Arrange fruit on a platter. Prepare Sesame-Lemon Dressing and pour into a small glass bowl for dipping. Garnish platter with mint and cherries. Serve with wooden picks for easy eating. Makes 8 servings.

Melon Balls

Fruit is always a welcome beginning to a meal.

1/2 medium-size cantaloupe
1/2 medium-size honeydew melon
1/4 cup Sherry-Lemon Dressing (page 29)
Mint sprigs

Using a melon baller, cut melons into balls. Combine melon balls in a medium-size bowl. Prepare dressing and pour over fruit. Cover and refrigerate several hours. Spoon into large chilled wine glasses or glass bowls. Garnish with mint. Makes 4 servings.

Guacamole

A very popular Southwestern dip. Serve with margaritas. Prepare just before serving, as avocados tend to brown.

2 ripe avocados, coarsely mashed
3 to 4 tablespoons fresh lemon juice
1 small tomato, peeled, seeded and
   finely chopped
2 finely chopped green onions, bulbs and
   2 inches of green tops
2 tablespoons fresh cilantro
1 garlic clove, minced
1/2 teaspoon chili powder
1/4 teaspoon hot pepper sauce
Salt
Freshly ground pepper
Corn chips

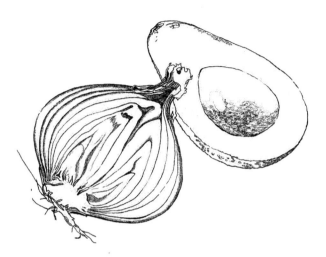

In a medium-size bowl, combine avocados and lemon juice. Mix in tomato, onions, cilantro, garlic, chili powder and hot pepper sauce. Season with salt and pepper to taste. Serve at room temperature with corn chips. Makes 2 cups.

Tip

Make your own low-calorie corn chips. Cut corn tortillas into 8 triangles. Let dry. Toast in a moderate oven until crisp.

Herb Dip

Dips are one of the most served hors d'oeuvres. They are easy to prepare ahead of time and always look attractive surrounded by an array of fresh vegetables or served with crisp crackers, bread sticks, chips or any of a variety of munchies.

1/2 cup dairy sour cream
1/2 cup cottage cheese
1/4 cup fresh lemon juice
1 tablespoon chopped fresh parsley
1 tablespoon chopped fresh chives
1 teaspoon dried leaf salad herbs, or a dash each
   of tarragon, thyme, basil and chervil
Salt
Freshly ground pepper

In a blender, process all ingredients. Season with salt and pepper to taste. Makes 1 cup.

Variations

Avocado Dip: Add 1 ripe mashed avocado.

Horseradish Dip: Add 1/4 cup prepared horseradish and 1/4 teaspoon paprika.

Mustard & Dill Dip: Add 2 to 3 tablespoons Dijon-style mustard and 1 tablespoon chopped fresh dill or 1 teaspoon dried dill.

Hummus

A very popular Mediterranean dish.

1/2 pound dried garbanzo beans, or 1 (8-oz.)
  can garbanzo beans
5 tablespoons fresh lemon juice
5 tablespoons extra-virgin olive oil
1/2 cup tahini paste (sesame paste)
2 garlic cloves, minced
1/8 teaspoon red (cayenne) pepper or to taste
Salt
Paprika
Parsley, chopped
8 to 10 Greek olives
Pita bread, cut into triangles

Cover beans with water and soak overnight. Drain beans. In a medium-size saucepan, cook beans in boiling water to cover 10 minutes. Reduce heat to medium and simmer beans 2 hours or until very tender. Drain well. Cool. If using canned beans, drain and rinse with cold water; drain again. Coarsely chop cooked beans in a blender. Add lemon juice, 3 tablespoons of the olive oil, the tahini paste, garlic and cayenne. Puree until finely blended. Mixture should have the consistency of mayonnaise. Salt to taste. To serve, spread hummus on a platter or serving plates. Smooth the surface. Hollow center and fill with remaining olive oil. Sprinkle top with paprika. Garnish with parsley and Greek olives. Serve with pita bread. Makes 4 or 5 servings.

Shrimp Cocktail

Serve individually as a first course, or arrange
on lettuce leaves on an iced platter as an hors d'oeuvre.

1/4 cup plain yogurt
2 tablespoons mayonnaise
3 tablespoons ketchup
2 tablespoons Worcestershire sauce
2 tablespoons fresh lemon juice
1 tablespoon prepared horseradish
1 teaspoon dry mustard
1 teaspoon freshly ground pepper
Shredded lettuce leaves
1 pound cooked large shrimp
4 to 6 thin lemon slices

In a medium-size bowl, combine yogurt, mayonnaise, ketchup, Worcestershire sauce, lemon juice, horseradish, mustard and pepper. Divide lettuce among 4 to 6 glass bowls or large wine glasses. Spoon sauce equally over lettuce. Arrange shrimp and a slice of lemon over edge of each bowl. Makes 4 to 6 servings.

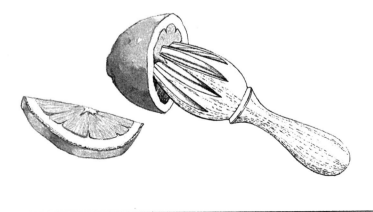

Shrimp Cocktail with Remoulade Sauce

This is a variation of the preceding Shrimp Cocktail.
This sauce is also excellent with cold poached fish.

Remoulade Sauce, see below
1 pound cooked large shrimp
4 to 6 thin lemon slices

Remoulade Sauce:

1 cup mayonnaise
1 tablespoon finely chopped green onion, bulb
   and 2 inches of green top
1 tablespoon prepared horseradish or to taste
1 teaspoon dry mustard
2 teaspoons minced fresh tarragon or 1/2
   teaspoon dried leaf tarragon
1 teaspoon fresh lemon juice or to taste
1 teaspoon grated lemon peel
1 bay leaf

Prepare Remoulade Sauce. Spoon sauce into centers of 4 to 6 small glass bowls. Arrange shrimp and a lemon slice over edge of each bowl. Makes 4 to 6 servings.

Remoulade Sauce

In a medium-size bowl, combine mayonnaise, green onion, horseradish, mustard, tarragon, lemon juice and lemon peel. Pour into a small container. Add bay leaf and refrigerate overnight. Remove bay leaf. Adjust horseradish and lemon juice to taste.

Vegetable Caviar

When the real thing just won't do.

1 large eggplant
3 green bell peppers
2 medium-size tomatoes
1 garlic clove, crushed
2 tablespoons extra-virgin olive oil
2 to 3 tablespoons fresh lemon juice
1 tablespoon white-wine vinegar
Salt
Freshly ground black pepper
Thin bread slices or triangles of pita
   bread, toasted

Preheat oven to 400°F (205°C). Arrange eggplant and bell peppers in a baking dish. Bake 15 to 20 minutes or until softened. Place into a paper bag; let stand 10 minutes. Place tomatoes in boiling water a few seconds, then place in iced water to cool. Remove skins and seeds from vegetables. Put vegetables and garlic into a blender. Process until chopped to a coarse consistency. Drain off excess liquid. Remove to a serving bowl. Combine olive oil, 2 tablespoons of the lemon juice and the vinegar. Pour over vegetables. Toss lightly. Season with salt and pepper to taste. Refrigerate several hours. Adjust lemon juice to taste. Serve with toast or pita bread. Makes 8 servings.

Variation

This dish makes an excellent salad served on a bed of lettuce. Garnish with parsley. Makes 4 servings.

Italian Cheese

Lemon and sesame seeds add a unique taste to a mild cheese.

1 pound mozzarella cheese
1/2 cup extra-virgin olive oil
1/3 cup plus 2 teaspoons fresh lemon juice
2 teaspoons sesame seeds
1 teaspoon grated lemon peel
Salt
Freshly ground pepper
1 small head radicchio
1/4 cup chopped sun-dried tomatoes
1 large red apple, thinly sliced
Parsley, to garnish
Ripe olives, to garnish
Plain crisp crackers

Slice cheese into thin rounds. In a small bowl, combine olive oil, the 1/3 cup lemon juice, sesame seeds and lemon peel. Season with salt and pepper to taste. Arrange radicchio leaves around rim of a large platter, leaving center open. Place a cheese round in each leaf and add 1 or 2 sun-dried tomato pieces. Drizzle dressing over cheese. Toss apple slices with remaining lemon juice. In center of platter arrange apples slices. Garnish with parsley and olives. Serve with crackers. Makes 8 to 10 servings.

OPEN-FACE SANDWICHES

Open-face sandwiches can be served on a variety of breads. The following are a few helpful suggestions:

- Spread on thinly sliced firm white bread with crust removed. Bread can be lightly toasted on one side.
- Spread on thinly sliced French, rye or dark pumpernickel bread, lightly toasted on one side.
- Spread on a variety of store-bought toasted bread rounds.
- Garnish plates with lemon slices, fresh parsley and thinly sliced red apples marinated in 1 tablespoon honey and 1 tablespoon lemon juice.

Crab with Avocado Open-face Sandwich

The lemon juice adds flavor and keeps the avocado from darkening.

1 large ripe avocado, mashed
1/4 cup fresh lemon juice
2 cups cooked crabmeat, flaked
1/3 cup dairy sour cream
1 teaspoon hot pepper sauce
1/2 teaspoon dried leaf thyme
4 thin black bread slices
4 parsley sprigs
4 thin lemon slices

In a medium-size bowl, combine avocado, lemon juice, crabmeat, sour cream, hot pepper sauce and thyme. Mound on bread. Garnish with parsley and lemon. Makes 4 open-face sandwiches or 2 servings.

Variation

Serve crabmeat mixture in lettuce cups. Garnish with cherry tomatoes. Accompany with dry toasted rye and pumpernickel rounds.

Curried Seafood Open-face Sandwich

Curry powder and cayenne add spice to a creamy filling.

6 ounces cooked crabmeat, lobster or shrimp
2 to 3 tablespoons mayonnaise
1 to 2 tablespoons fresh lemon juice
1 tablespoon minced fresh chives
1/4 teaspoon curry powder
1/8 teaspoon red (cayenne) pepper
4 bread slices
4 thin Cheddar cheese, Swiss cheese or Monterey
   Jack cheese slices

In a medium-size bowl, combine shellfish, mayonnaise, lemon juice, chives, curry powder and cayenne. Spread over bread. Top with cheese. Broil until cheese just begins to bubble. Makes 4 open-face sandwiches or 2 servings.

Variations

Substitute 1 cup diced cooked chicken or turkey for seafood. Cut sandwiches into quarters for a hot hors d'oeuvre.

Tuna Open-face Sandwich

Sunflower kernels add a crunchy flavor surprise.

1 (6-oz.) can tuna or salmon, drained
1/4 cup finely chopped celery
3 to 4 tablespoons mayonnaise
2 tablespoons fresh lemon juice
1 tablespoon finely chopped green onion, white
   part only
2 tablespoons sunflower kernels
4 bread slices
4 cucumber or tomato slices
2 lemon slices

In a medium-size bowl, flake tuna or salmon with a fork. Add celery, mayonnaise, lemon juice, green onion and sunflower kernels; stir until combined. Spread over bread. Top with cucumber or tomato. Garnish with lemon slices. Makes 4 open-face sandwiches or 2 servings.

Variation

Substitute 1 cup diced cooked chicken or turkey for tuna or salmon.

Salads

Salads are classic favorites and we have tried to include some of the most popular, with a lemon twist. There are recipes for vegetable salads, pasta salads and rice salads that can be served as delicious side dishes or main courses.

It is surprising how easy salad dressings are to make and how creative you feel when making them. Lemon juice can be substituted for vinegar in almost any salad dressing.

QUICK SALAD TIPS

- Most foods, including meats, fish, pastas, fruits and vegetables, can be used in salads. One can be as creative as one's imagination. Whether you prepare a simple or complex salad, choose foods that complement each other. Lemon peel always makes an attractive garnish. A squeeze of lemon juice brightens and freshens all types of salads.
- Rub or dip peeled apples, avocados, bananas and pineapple in fresh lemon juice to prevent browning.
- Serve a simple green salad lightly coated in oil with just a squeeze of lemon, seasoned with salt and pepper to taste.
- Create your own dressings. They are very simple to prepare and superior to any store-bought dressing. (You will wonder why you ever used prepared dressings.)
- When making dressings for fruit salads, combine in the ratio of 1 tablespoon lemon juice to 1 tablespoon honey, or combine in ratio of 1 tablespoon lemon juice to 1/4 cup whipping cream. Add sugar to taste. Add any of the variety of dessert or sweet spices to either dressing: allspice, cinnamon, ginger, mint, nutmeg and mace.

- When making dressings for meat or fish salads, combine whipping cream and fresh lemon juice in the proportions listed on opposite page, delete sugar and add salt and freshly ground pepper to taste. Add mustard, dill or horseradish.
- For vegetable salads, create your own vinaigrette, which despite its name can be made with lemon juice in part or in whole. Combine in a ratio of 2 tablespoons lemon juice to 1/4 cup oil or 1 tablespoon lemon juice and 1 tablespoon vinegar to 1/4 cup oil. Season with salt and pepper to taste. Add any of a variety of herbs and spices of your choice and add such ingredients as garlic, mustard, pureed greens or tomatoes, onions, pickles, capers, anchovies, grated cheese, sardines and hard-cooked egg yolks.
- Toss salads lightly with flat wooden spoons or gently with your hands, turning salad from bottom to top so that all ingredients are evenly coated with dressing. Give the salad enough room in the bowl to toss with ease.
- It is better to serve salads in glass, pottery or porcelain salad bowls that can be thoroughly cleaned. Wood salad bowls are porous and cannot be cleaned properly and over time, as oils stick, they become rancid.
- The most important rule in preparing salads is to use only top quality ingredients and the very freshest produce. Buy what is in season. Remember, your salad is only as good as the ingredients you put into it.

Cole Slaw

Pack slaw in your picnic basket with a variety of sandwiches—turkey, roast beef, corned beef and salami. It's also great with a glass of beer, barbecued hamburgers and frankfurters.

1 small green cabbage head
2 tablespoons green onion, white part only
1 teaspoon salt
Dash of freshly ground pepper
3 carrots, grated
1 green bell pepper, cut into thin strips
1/4 cup dairy sour cream
1/4 cup mayonnaise
4 tablespoons fresh lemon juice
1 to 3 teaspoons sugar
1/4 teaspoon hot pepper sauce
1-1/2 teaspoons caraway seeds (optional)

Soak cabbage in iced water 1 hour. Dry in a vegetable spinner or pat dry with paper towels. Sprinkle with onion, salt and pepper. Add carrots and bell pepper. Refrigerate until ready to serve. In a small bowl, combine sour cream, mayonnaise, 2 tablespoons of the lemon juice, 1 teaspoon of the sugar, the hot pepper sauce and caraway seeds, if using. Pour over slaw and toss lightly. Add remaining lemon juice and sugar to taste. Makes 4 servings.

Greek Salad

The classic Mediterranean salad. Serve with your
favorite soup and thick bread for lunch or a light supper.

1 cucumber, peeled, seeded and diced
1 green bell pepper, cut into thin rings
12 Greek olives
1 tablespoon finely chopped fresh parsley
1/4 pound feta cheese, diced
1/4 cup extra-virgin olive oil
3 tablespoons fresh lemon juice
1 small garlic clove, crushed (optional)
1/2 teaspoon dried leaf oregano
Salt
Freshly ground black pepper
Lettuce leaves
2 small tomatoes, cut into quarters
4 to 8 anchovy fillets, rinsed and patted dry
   (optional)
Parsley sprigs, to garnish

In a large bowl, combine cucumber, bell pepper, olives, chopped parsley and cheese. In a small bowl, blend olive oil, lemon juice, garlic, oregano, salt and black pepper. Pour over salad. Toss lightly. Arrange lettuce on chilled individual salad plates and top with salad. Place tomato wedges and 1 or 2 anchovy fillets, if desired, on each plate. Garnish with parsley sprigs. Makes 4 servings.

Potato Salad

Always the right salad for picnics or the family's outdoor barbecue.

4 medium-size potatoes
2 tablespoons chopped green onion, bulb and
   1/3 green leaves
1/3 to 1/2 cup extra-virgin olive oil
1/4 cup plus 1 tablespoon fresh lemon juice
1 tablespoon chopped fresh parsley
1/4 teaspoon paprika
2 teaspoons capers (optional)
Salt
Freshly ground pepper
1 hard-cooked egg yolk, crumbled
2 hard-cooked eggs, quartered
4 green olives and 4 ripe olives

Scrub potatoes and score completely around center with point of a sharp knife. In a large saucepan, boil potatoes in salted water until tender, but firm. Drain. Return to low heat. Shake pan while heating 1 to 2 minutes to remove all moisture from potatoes. Remove potatoes with a slotted spoon. Cool. Peel off skins and cut into medium-size cubes. Combine in a serving bowl with onion. In a blender, process oil, lemon juice, parsley and paprika until well blended. Stir in capers, if using. Pour dressing over potatoes and toss lightly. Season with salt and pepper to taste. Refrigerate several hours. Before serving sprinkle salad with crumbled egg yolk. Garnish with eggs and olives. Makes 4 servings.

Variation

Substitute 1/3 to 1/2 cup mayonnaise or 3 to 4 tablespoons mayonnaise and 3 to 4 tablespoons sour cream for oil. Combine dressing ingredients in a small bowl until well blended.

Spinach & Cucumber Salad

An elegant, easy-to-prepare salad with a
simple dressing that will add zest to any dinner.

1-1/2 pounds spinach
2 cucumbers, peeled, seeded and thinly sliced
1 cup thinly sliced celery
2/3 cup small ripe olives
1/3 cup pine nuts or sunflower kernels
1/3 cup chopped fresh dill (optional)
Lemon-Raspberry Dressing, see below
Pimentos (optional)
1 hard-cooked egg yolk, crumbled (optional)

Lemon-Raspberry Dressing:
1/2 cup extra-virgin olive oil
2 tablespoons fresh lemon juice
2 tablespoons raspberry vinegar
1 teaspoon salt
1/2 teaspoon dried leaf tarragon
1/4 teaspoon freshly ground pepper

Wash spinach thoroughly. Pat dry. If leaves are large, tear in half. In a salad bowl, combine spinach, cucumbers, celery, olives, nuts and dill, if using. Prepare dressing and pour over salad. Toss lightly. Garnish with several pimentos or egg yolk, if desired. Makes 4 to 6 servings.

Lemon-Raspberry Dressing
Process all ingredients in a blender until combined.

Tabbouleh

*A great salad or side dish that has become very
popular with the diet and health conscious crowd.*

1-1/2 cups bulgur wheat
3 cups boiling water
3/4 cup chopped green onions
3/4 cup chopped green bell pepper
1/2 English cucumber, diced
3/4 cup chopped fresh parsley
1/4 cup chopped fresh mint or 4 teaspoons dried
    leaf mint
1/4 cup pine nuts
2 tablespoons sliced Greek olives
1/3 cup fresh lemon juice
1/3 cup extra-virgin olive oil
1/4 teaspoon freshly ground black pepper
Salt
Lettuce leaves
2 medium-size tomatoes, quartered, or
    12 cherry tomatoes
Parsley sprigs

In a medium-size saucepan, combine bulgur and water. Boil 15 minutes or cook according to package directions. Drain. Pat dry between paper towels, removing all excess water. Cool. In a large bowl, combine bulgur, onions, bell pepper, cucumber, parsley, mint, nuts and olives. Add lemon juice, olive oil and black pepper. Toss lightly. Season with salt to taste. Refrigerate several hours, tossing occasionally. Line a serving bowl with lettuce leaves. Spoon salad into lettuce-lined bowl. Add tomatoes and parsley sprigs. Makes 6 servings.

Rice Salad with Honey-Lemon Dressing

*A very refreshing, decorative salad for a summer
meal. Makes a lovely centerpiece for an outdoor brunch.*

2 cups hot cooked rice
1 tablespoon butter or margarine
1 tangerine, sectioned, or 1/2 cup canned
   mandarin oranges
1/2 cup pineapple chunks, fresh or canned
1/2 cup sliced strawberries
1/4 cup halved pecans
Honey-Lemon Dressing, see below
6 to 8 whole strawberries

Honey-Lemon Dressing:
1/4 cup vegetable oil, preferably canola oil
3 tablespoons honey
3 tablespoons fresh lemon juice
1/2 teaspoon dry mustard
1/2 teaspoon salt

Toss hot rice with butter and allow to cool. When rice is cold, add tangerine, pineapple, sliced strawberries and pecans. Prepare Honey-Lemon Dressing and pour over rice mixture. Toss well. Garnish with whole strawberries. Makes 6 to 8 servings.

Honey-Lemon Dressing
Combine all ingredients in a small bowl until well blended.

Vegetable Salad

Serve as a main dish for lunch or as a light supper with French bread.
Can be made in large quantities for a party. Keeps well in the refrigerator for several days.

1 cucumber, peeled, seeded and cut into
   1/4-inch cubes
2 medium-size zucchini, halved, cut into
   1/4-inch slices
3/4 cup carrots, cut into 1/4-inch rounds
2 medium-size red potatoes
1 red or green bell pepper, cut into thin strips
3/4 cup frozen green peas, thawed
3/4 cup canned whole-kernel corn
1/2 cup pine nuts or sunflower kernels
1/4 cup coarsely chopped green onions
6 to 8 each green and ripe olives, thinly sliced
3/4 to 1 cup French Dressing (page 32)
1/2 cup plain yogurt
1/2 cup dairy sour cream
1/4 cup fresh lemon juice
Salt
Freshly ground black pepper
Lettuce leaves
8 whole olives, to garnish

In a small bowl, sprinkle cucumbers with salt and weight with a heavy saucepan or bowl. In a medium-size saucepan, steam zucchini and carrots until just crisp-tender. Remove from heat and cool under cold water. Scrub potatoes thoroughly. With a sharp knife score around each potato. Cook potatoes in boiling water until tender. Drain and cool. Peel potatoes and cut into small cubes. Drain cucumbers and press between paper towels to remove as much moisture as possible. In a large bowl, combine cucumber, zucchini, carrots, potatoes, bell pepper, peas, corn, pine nuts, onions and sliced olives. Pour French Dressing over vegetables and marinate for several hours in refrigerator, tossing occasionally. Drain vegetables with a slotted spoon. In a small bowl, combine yogurt, sour cream and lemon juice. Pour over vegetables. Toss salad. Season with salt and black pepper to taste. Line salad plates with lettuce leaves. Spoon salad over lettuce. Garnish with whole olives. Makes 8 servings.

Variations

Substitute mayonnaise for yogurt.

Chicken or Turkey Vegetable Salad: Substitute mayonnaise for yogurt. Add 1 tablespoon fresh dill or 1 teaspoon dried dill and 1/4 teaspoon dry mustard to mayonnaise. Toss 1-1/2 cups julienned cooked chicken or turkey in mayonnaise.

Shrimp Vegetable Salad: Substitute mayonnaise for yogurt. Add 1/8 teaspoon red (cayenne) pepper to mayonnaise. Toss 1-3/4 cups baby shrimp in mayonnaise. Add 1/4 cup sliced celery to vegetables. Serve with lemon slices.

Vegetable Salad in Tomato Cups: Reduce amounts for vegetable salad by half. Place 8 medium-size tomatoes in boiling water to loosen skins, then in iced water to cool. Remove skin. Cut tops off tomatoes and scoop out insides. Turn tomatoes upside down to drain. Pat dry with paper towels. Refrigerate several hours. Add 1/2 teaspoon dried leaf basil to yogurt mixture. Spoon vegetables into tomatoes. Allow a little salad to spill over sides.

Crab Pasta Salad

This pasta dish is dedicated to the lemon lovers who like their salads tangy.

1/2 pound flat noodles (linguine or fettuccine)
1/3 to 1/2 cup extra-virgin olive oil
6 ounces cooked crabmeat, flaked
1 tablespoon mayonnaise
3/4 to 1 pound fresh asparagus
About 1/3 cup fresh lemon juice
2 tablespoons white-wine vinegar
1 teaspoon Dijon-style mustard
1/2 teaspoon sugar
Salt
Freshly ground pepper
1 teaspoon grated lemon peel

Cook noodles according to package directions. Rinse under cold water. Drain. Place in a serving dish and toss lightly with 1/4 cup of the oil. Combine crabmeat and mayonnaise. Add to noodles. Cut off bottoms and scales on asparagus stalks. Peel 1/3 of the way up the stalk. Cut into 1-inch pieces. Steam asparagus until just tender. Marinate in 1/4 cup lemon juice 15 minutes. Remove from juice. Reserve juice. Combine noodle mixture with asparagus. In a small bowl, combine remaining olive oil, reserved lemon juice, vinegar, mustard and sugar. Season with salt and pepper to taste. Pour dressing over noodles and toss lightly. Refrigerate until served. Just before serving, add remaining lemon juice to taste. Sprinkle lemon peel over top. Makes 3 or 4 servings.

Gingered Vegetable Pasta Salad

Pasta, pasta, pasta—the dish of the late 1980s is going strong in the 90s.

1/2 pound tubular noodles (rigatoni or macaroni)
2 tablespoons peanut oil
1 (2- to 3-inch) piece gingerroot
1 cup chopped celery
3/4 cup sliced carrots
1/2 pound snow peas
1 green, red or yellow bell pepper, cut into
     thin strips
1/4 cup pine nuts or sunflower kernels
3 to 5 tablespoons fresh lemon juice
1 to 2 teaspoons honey
Salt
Freshly ground pepper
1 teaspoon grated lemon peel

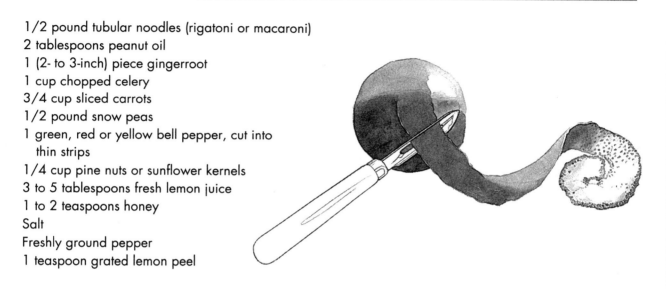

Cook noodles according to package directions. Rinse under cold water. Drain. Place in a serving dish and toss lightly with oil. Peel gingerroot. Cut into chunks. Using a garlic press, squeeze out 2 to 3 tablespoons ginger juice. In a medium-size saucepan, steam celery and carrots 3 minutes. Cut ends and strings off peas. Add peas and steam another 3 minutes. Rinse vegetables under cold water to cool; drain. Add to pasta. Add ginger juice, bell pepper and pine nuts to pasta. Combine 2 tablespoons of the lemon juice and the honey. Add to pasta. Season with salt and pepper to taste. Add remaining lemon juice to taste. Refrigerate until chilled. Garnish with lemon peel. Makes 3 or 4 servings.

Dilled Cucumbers

Makes a great side dish. Serve with almost any fish dish, roasted turkey or chicken.

3 cucumbers, peeled, seeded, quartered and
  thinly sliced
1/2 teaspoon salt
2 to 3 tablespoons fresh lemon juice
2 tablespoons champagne vinegar
2 to 3 teaspoons sugar
2 tablespoons chopped fresh dill or 2 teaspoons
  dried dill
Freshly ground pepper
1/4 cup plain yogurt (optional)

In a small bowl, sprinkle cucumbers with salt and weight with a heavy saucepan or bowl. Refrigerate 3 to 4 hours. Drain. Press cucumbers between paper towels to remove as much moisture as possible. Combine 2 tablespoons of the lemon juice, the vinegar, 2 teaspoons of the sugar, the dill, pepper and yogurt, if using. Pour over cucumbers and toss gently. Refrigerate 2 hours before serving. Add remaining lemon juice and sugar to taste. Makes 4 servings.

Variation

Cucumbers with Almonds: Delete dill and add 1/4 cup toasted chopped almonds. Substitute 1-1/2 large English cucumbers for the 3 cucumbers. Thinly slice unpeeled cucumbers.

Sesame-Lemon Dressing

This dressing is excellent with any fruit salad.

1/2 cup sesame seeds
1 cup plain yogurt
4 to 5 tablespoons fresh lemon juice
2 to 3 tablespoons honey

Toast sesame seeds in a dry skillet over medium heat. Combine all ingredients in a blender and blend until almost smooth and creamy. (The sesame seeds will give the dressing a slight textured look and feel.) Makes 1 cup.

Variation

Substitute 1 cup whipping cream for yogurt.

Sherry-Lemon Dressing

Here is a tart dressing to be poured over fruit or tossed with a fruit salad. There is no oil, so it is low in calories.

1/4 cup fresh lemon juice
2 tablespoons honey
2 tablespoons cream sherry
1/2 teaspoon poppy seeds

In a small bowl, combine lemon juice and honey until well blended. Stir in sherry and poppy seeds. Refrigerate until served. Makes 1/2 cup.

Blue Cheese Dressing

A low-calorie version of an old favorite.

1/4 cup nonfat plain yogurt
2 to 3 tablespoons fresh lemon juice
1 teaspoon sugar
1/2 teaspoon dried leaf tarragon
1/2 teaspoon salt
Freshly ground pepper
1 garlic clove (optional), crushed
1/4 cup crumbled blue cheese

In a blender, combine yogurt, lemon juice, sugar, tarragon, salt, pepper and garlic, if using. Blend until smooth and creamy. Add cheese to blended ingredients. Refrigerate until served. Makes 3/4 cup.

Variation

Add 2 tablespoons mayonnaise to cheese. Combine with blended ingredients. This makes a thicker, creamier dressing with a few more calories.

Broccoli Dressing

Serve on mixed green salads with cherry tomatoes on the side for color.

1 cup chopped cooked broccoli
1/4 cup extra-virgin olive oil
2 tablespoons fresh lemon juice
2 tablespoons white-wine vinegar
1/2 teaspoon salad herbs or a dash each of dried
   leaf basil, tarragon and thyme
1/8 teaspoon dill
1/8 teaspoon dry mustard
1/8 teaspoon salt
Freshly ground pepper
1/2 teaspoon sesame seeds

Blend all ingredients, except sesame seeds, in a blender until almost creamy. Add sesame seeds. Refrigerate until served. Makes 3/4 cup.

French Dressing

Classic French dressing with a lemon twist.

1/2 cup extra-virgin olive oil
3 tablespoons fresh lemon juice
2 tablespoons white-wine vinegar
1 small garlic clove, crushed
1/2 teaspoon sugar
1/4 teaspoon dry mustard
1/4 teaspoon paprika
1/4 teaspoon dried leaf chervil
1/4 teaspoon dried leaf tarragon
1/8 teaspoon dried leaf thyme
1/8 teaspoon dried leaf basil
1/2 teaspoon salt
Freshly ground pepper

Combine all ingredients in a blender, using 2 tablespoons of the lemon juice, and blend until smooth and creamy. Add remaining lemon juice to taste. Makes 3/4 cup.

Green Goddess Dressing

Serve on cold vegetables, mixed green salads or cold fish.

1/4 cup plain yogurt
1/4 cup chopped fresh parsley
1 green onion, chopped
2 tablespoons fresh lemon juice
2 tablespoons white-wine vinegar
1/2 teaspoon salt
1/2 teaspoon salad herbs or dash each of dried
   leaf basil, tarragon and thyme
1/4 teaspoon freshly ground pepper
1/2 cup mayonnaise

Process all ingredients, except mayonnaise, in a blender until smooth. Stir in mayonnaise. Refrigerate until served. Makes 3/4 cup.

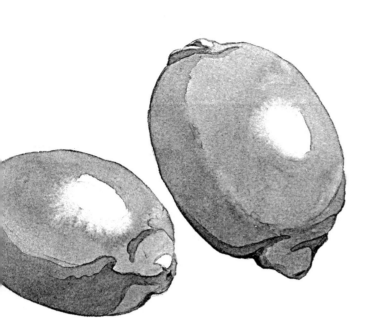

Main Dishes

Lemon complements many of the ingredients found in main dishes, including seafood, beef, veal, poultry, cheese and vegetables. For example, it's hard to imagine shrimp without lemon juice or fresh fish served without a lemon wedge.

Poultry seems to be the protein of choice these days and I have included a variety of poultry recipes that are enhanced by the careful use of lemon.

Carbohydrate-packed pasta can be made into delicious vegetarian main dishes or combined with seafood, meat or poultry. Pasta benefits from marinating in lemon dressing and sauces.

Creamy Lemon Pasta

*This also makes a great side dish. It's easy to prepare and
delicious to eat. Be sure to pass the Parmesan cheese and the pepper grinder.*

1 pound pasta
2 cups whipping cream
1 to 2 tablespoons grated lemon peel
1/4 pound freshly grated Parmesan cheese
Freshly ground pepper

Cook noodles according to package directions. Drain and place in a bowl. In a medium-size skillet over low heat, heat cream and lemon peel, stirring, 5 minutes. Do not boil. When hot, pour over cooked pasta and toss to combine. Serve with Parmesan cheese and freshly ground pepper. Makes 4 to 6 servings.

Variation

Add 2 tablespoons capers or 1/2 cup chopped ripe olives.

Three-Mushroom Pasta

The variety of mushrooms used give this dish its distinct flavor. This is a great alternative to a red pasta sauce. A hot crusty baguette is the perfect accompaniment.

1 tablespoon butter or margarine
1 tablespoon extra-virgin olive oil
3 garlic cloves, minced
1/4 cup diced shallots
2 cups button mushrooms, cut into quarters
1-1/2 cups oyster mushrooms, cut into
   1/4-inch slices
1-1/2 cups shiitake mushrooms, cut into
   1/4-inch slices
1/2 cup white wine
1/3 cup fresh lemon juice
1 teaspoon grated lemon peel
1/2 teaspoon dried leaf thyme
1/2 cup sliced ripe olives
1 (14-oz.) can chicken broth
1 pound linguine
1/4 cup grated Parmesan cheese
Freshly ground pepper

In a large skillet, heat butter and oil over medium-high heat. Add garlic and shallots. Cook 2 minutes. Add mushrooms and cook 5 to 7 minutes, stirring occasionally, until limp. Add wine, lemon juice, lemon peel, thyme, olives and chicken broth. Bring to a boil. Reduce heat to a simmer. Cover and cook 30 minutes. Cook linguine according to package directions. Drain and return to pot. Pour sauce over pasta and let sit, covered, 10 minutes. Add Parmesan cheese and toss to combine. Season with pepper to taste. Makes 4 to 6 servings.

Pasta with Lemon

Try it! You'll like it! Use your favorite type of pasta.

1/3 cup extra-virgin olive oil
2 medium-size onions, coarsely chopped
1/4 cup fresh lemon juice
2 teaspoons sugar
1 tablespoon grated lemon peel
1 pound pasta
1/4 to 1/3 cup freshly grated Parmesan cheese
Salt
Freshly ground pepper
1 tablespoon finely chopped chives or
   green onion

In a medium-size skillet over medium heat, heat 2 tablespoons of the oil. Add onions and sauté until softened. Add lemon juice, sugar and lemon peel. Cook 1 minute. Cook pasta according to package directions. Drain and toss in a large bowl with sautéed onions, 2 tablespoons of the cheese and remaining oil. Season with salt and pepper to taste. Garnish with chives and remaining cheese. Makes 4 to 6 servings.

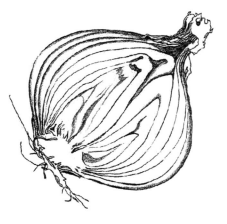

Red Pepper & Tri-colored Lemon Pasta

The varied colors of this dish and the subtle hint of lemon make a delicious and eye-appealing dish. This pasta can be served hot for dinner or at room temperature for lunch.

3 red bell peppers
1/2 cup extra-virgin olive oil
2 tablespoons finely chopped garlic
1 to 2 tablespoons grated lemon peel
1 pound tri-colored rotelle pasta
1/4 to 1/3 cup freshly grated Parmesan cheese
Freshly ground black pepper

Preheat broiler. Wash and core peppers. Cut peppers in half and place peppers skin-side up on a broiler pan. Broil peppers until blistered and blackened, 5 to 10 minutes. Place in a plastic bag and cool 10 minutes. Peel peppers. Reserve juice. Cut peppers into 1/4-inch slices. In a large skillet over medium-low heat, heat oil. Add garlic and sauté 10 to 15 minutes. Add lemon peel and cook 1 minute. Add peppers and reserved juice and cook 5 minutes. Prepare pasta according to package directions. Drain and place in a large serving bowl. Pour sauce over pasta and toss to combine. Serve with cheese and black pepper. Makes 4 to 6 servings.

Spaghettini with Zucchini

Serve with crisp sourdough bread and a glass of white wine.

3 tablespoons extra-virgin olive oil
4 small zucchini, cut into 1/2-inch rounds
1/2 teaspoon minced shallots
1/4 teaspoon dried leaf thyme
1/3 cup dry white wine
1/3 cup fresh lemon juice
1/2 cup plus 1 tablespoon whipping cream
1 (12-oz.) package spaghettini
2 tablespoons finely chopped fresh parsley
Freshly grated Parmesan cheese

In a medium-size skillet over medium heat, heat oil. Add zucchini, shallots and thyme and sauté until zucchini is crisp-tender. Remove zucchini with a slotted spoon. Add wine and lemon juice to skillet and simmer several minutes until liquid is reduced to half. Over low heat, stir in cream and simmer, stirring occasionally, until sauce thickens. Cook spaghettini according to package directions; drain. Combine spaghettini and zucchini in a large serving bowl. Pour sauce over spaghettini. Sprinkle with parsley and Parmesan cheese. Makes 4 to 6 servings.

QUICK TIPS FOR PREPARING FISH

- Fish can be prepared by steaming, poaching, broiling, baking, grilling, sautéing and deep-frying. No matter how fish is prepared, lemon is the perfect complement. A squeeze of lemon before preparing will enhance the flavor of any fish.
- A dash of grated lemon peel on prepared fish will add fragrance and color.
- When serving fish, garnish each plate with a lemon slice.
- When broiling a whole fish, place 2 to 3 thin lemon slices inside the cavity.
- Broiled fish should be prepared by cooking 10 minutes to the inch, measured at its thickest point, 3 to 4 inches from the heating element. For example, fresh fish, 1 inch thick, at room temperature would be broiled 5 minutes on each side. Add an additional 2 minutes for fish direct from refrigerator.
- Fillets should be broiled from 1-1/2 to 3 minutes on each side depending on thickness.
- When preparing frozen fish, double cooking time, 20 minutes to the inch.
- Baked fish should be cooked at 450°F (230°C), 5 minutes to the inch.
- When broiling fish, preheat broiler 10 minutes. Lightly oil broiler pan to prevent fish from sticking.
- Fish covered in foil should be baked 5 minutes longer if fresh, 10 minutes if frozen, to allow heat to penetrate foil.
- Fish is done when it is slightly shiny, opaque and begins to flake when pierced with a knife or a fork.

Halibut with Mushrooms in Cream Sauce

*A gourmet dish made simple. Serve with a grilled tomato, French
bread and a dry white wine and voilà, a main course fit for royalty.*

1/2 cup dry white wine
3 tablespoons fresh lemon juice
2 teaspoons finely chopped fresh parsley
1 pound halibut, cut 1 inch thick
1 tablespoon butter
4 to 5 medium-size mushrooms, finely diced
1 tablespoon finely chopped green onion, bulb
   and 1/3 of green tops
2 to 3 tablespoons whipping cream
Salt
Freshly ground pepper

Combine wine, 2 tablespoons of the lemon juice and parsley in a small poacher or a medium-size skillet and bring to a brisk boil. Reduce heat to simmer and poach halibut in liquid, 10 minutes or until fish turns from translucent to opaque. Place on a serving dish. Cover fish to keep warm. Reserve liquid. In a heavy skillet, over medium heat, melt butter. Add mushrooms and onion. Sauté until just tender, 3 to 4 minutes. Add reserved liquid and cook over high heat, stirring constantly with a wire whisk, until liquid disappears. Reduce heat to low. Add cream and remaining lemon juice and cook, stirring constantly, until sauce is smooth and creamy. Season with salt and pepper to taste. Pour over fish. Makes 2 servings.

Variation

To reduce calories and cholesterol, substitute 2 to 3 tablespoons of plain yogurt for whipping cream. Omit lemon juice added to cream.

Herbed Baked Fish

This recipe works well for a variety of fish: halibut,
white fish, swordfish, salmon or whatever is fresh and available.

2 pounds fish steaks, 1 inch thick
Marinade, see below
4 lemon slices
Parsley sprigs

Marinade:
1/4 cup vegetable oil
1/4 cup dry white wine
1/4 cup fresh lemon juice
1 teaspoon grated lemon peel
1 tablespoon chopped fresh parsley
3/4 teaspoon freshly ground black pepper
1/4 teaspoon salt (optional)
1/8 teaspoon red (cayenne) pepper (optional)
Dash each of dried leaf oregano, tarragon
    and thyme

Place fish in a shallow baking dish. Prepare Marinade. Pour over fish and turn to coat. Marinate 1 hour at room temperature, turning occasionally. Preheat oven to 450°F (230°C). Cover fish and bake 10 minutes. With a broad spatula, turn fish. Bake, uncovered, 5 minutes or until fish turns from translucent to opaque. Spoon liquid over fish. Serve with lemon slices. Garnish with parsley. Makes 3 or 4 servings.

Marinade

In a small bowl, combine all ingredients until well blended.

Variation

Herbed Broiled Fish: Preheat broiler 10 minutes. Lightly oil a broiler pan. Place fish on broiler pan. Brush with Marinade. Broil fish steaks 3 inches from heating element, 5 minutes per side. Brush with Marinade again after turning fish.

Shrimp & Mushrooms with Rice

A meal-in-one. Serve with a green salad and fresh fruit for dessert.

Lemon-Butter Rice (page 66)
1 pound mushrooms
1 tablespoon vegetable oil
1/4 cup coarsely chopped onion
1 tablespoon curry powder
Dash of hot pepper sauce
Dash of Worcestershire sauce
1/4 cup chopped fresh or canned tomatoes
1 pound large cooked shrimp
Salt

Prepare Lemon-Butter Rice. Clean mushrooms and remove stems. In a large skillet over medium heat, heat oil. Add onion and sauté until soft. Add curry powder, hot pepper sauce, Worcestershire sauce and tomatoes. Cover and simmer 15 to 20 minutes. Add mushroom caps. Simmer, uncovered, several minutes. Add shrimp and heat 1 minute. Add salt to taste. Serve shrimp and mushrooms over rice. Makes 4 servings.

Marinated White Fish

A cold fish dish that can be prepared in advance, this also makes a great first course.

2 pounds white fish fillets, 1 inch thick
2 to 3 tablespoons fresh lemon juice
All-purpose flour
2 tablespoons vegetable oil
6 tablespoons butter or margarine
Marinade, see below
Olives
Lemon slices
1/4 teaspoon dry mustard
Green Goddess Dressing (page 33)

Marinade:
1/2 cup extra-virgin olive oil
1/4 cup fresh lemon juice
1/4 cup fresh orange juice
1/4 cup finely chopped fresh shallots or 4
   teaspoons dried shallots
2 tablespoons finely chopped fresh cilantro
1/8 teaspoon red (cayenne) pepper

Dip fish in lemon juice and roll in flour until well-coated. In a large skillet over medium heat, heat oil and butter. Add fish and fry 5 to 8 minutes on each side until light golden-brown. Place fish in a deep serving dish. Let cool. Prepare Marinade and pour over fish. Refrigerate overnight. To serve, garnish with olives and lemon slices. Stir mustard into dressing and serve with fish. Makes 4 to 6 servings.

Marinade

In a small bowl, combine all ingredients and blend thoroughly.

Hint

Try either filleted Chilean sea bass or halibut depending on taste. The sea bass is richer and fattier than the halibut.

White Fish Fillets

Serve with a green salad and steamed rice.

1 lemon, thinly sliced
2 tablespoons water
1 pound white fish or sole fillets
3 tablespoons fresh lemon juice
All-purpose flour
1 egg, slightly beaten
Bread crumbs
1 tablespoon vegetable oil
4 tablespoons butter
1/2 cup dry white wine
1 teaspoon dried leaf tarragon
Parsley sprigs

In a small saucepan over low heat, simmer lemon slices in water 5 minutes. Meanwhile, dip fillets in 2 tablespoons of the lemon juice, then dredge in flour. Dip fillets in egg, then roll in bread crumbs. In a large skillet over medium heat, heat oil and 3 tablespoons of the butter. Add fillets and fry on each side 2 to 3 minutes. Transfer to a warm platter. Add remaining butter and lemon juice, the wine and tarragon to lemon slices. Simmer until sauce is reduced to half. Pour over fish. Arrange lemon slices on fish. Garnish with parsley. Makes 2 or 3 servings.

Italian Garnish

Use this to garnish meats or poultry.

1 medium-size garlic clove, coarsely chopped
1 tablespoon grated lemon peel
1/2 cup chopped curly parsley or Italian parsley

In a small bowl, combine all ingredients. Seal in a plastic bag. Refrigerate up to 3 to 5 days. Add to meats or poultry just before serving. Makes about 1/2 cup.

QUICK TIPS FOR USING LEMONS WITH MEAT & POULTRY

The acidity of lemon juice acts as both a flavor enhancer and a tenderizer.
- Use fresh lemon juice in marinades prepared for meat or poultry.
- Rub a small amount of lemon juice on raw poultry or game.
- When roasting poultry, insert 1 to 2 lemon slices in the cavity.
- When preparing burgers, add 1 teaspoon lemon juice per pound to ground meat or ground poultry.

Sauerbraten

This is a hearty main dish. Serve with noodles,
a steamed green vegetable and a full-bodied Burgundy.

4 pounds beef brisket
Salt
Pepper
Marinade, see below
All-purpose flour
2 tablespoons vegetable oil
16 pitted prunes
6 Italian plum tomatoes, quartered
1 (6-oz.) can tomato paste
1/2 cup firmly packed brown sugar
Parsley sprigs

Marinade:
2 cups water
1 cup fresh lemon juice
1 cup cider vinegar
1 onion, sliced
1/2 cup firmly packed brown sugar
1 bay leaf

Place meat in a large bowl. Season with salt and pepper. Prepare Marinade. Pour over meat. Cover and refrigerate 24 hours or longer. Separately, remove meat and onions. Pat meat dry with paper towels. Dredge in flour. In a large heavy pot over medium-high heat, heat oil and brown meat on all sides. Add onions and brown onions lightly. Add prunes, tomatoes, 1-1/2 cups of the Marinade, the tomato paste and 1 tablespoon of the brown sugar. Cover and simmer over low heat until meat is tender, 2 to 2-1/2 hours. To test for tenderness, insert the point of a sharp knife into meat. It should give easily. Remove meat to a cutting board. If cooking liquid is too thin for sauce, thicken with a little flour. Taste sauce and add remaining brown sugar as needed. Sauce should have a definite sweet and sour taste. Simmer sauce

10 minutes, stirring occasionally. When meat is cool enough to handle, cut into thin slices. Return to pot. Simmer 5 minutes. Place beef on platter. Pour some sauce over meat. Garnish with parsley. Serve extra sauce in a gravy boat. Makes 8 servings.

Marinade

In a medium-size saucepan, combine all ingredients. Bring to a boil, stirring until sugar dissolves. Cool.

Steak au Poivre

Beef today is 20 percent leaner than it was 20 years ago. This makes those who are steak lovers able to indulge on occasion without guilt.

2 tablespoons peppercorns
4 beef club steaks, 1-1/2 inches thick
1 to 2 teaspoons salt
1 tablespoon vegetable oil
5 teaspoons butter
1 teaspoon Worcestershire sauce
1/4 cup fresh lemon juice
2 tablespoons cognac
2 tablespoons chopped fresh chives or 2
    tablespoons chopped fresh parsley
1/4 cup lemon marmalade (optional)

Crush peppercorns with a rolling pin or the bottom of a heavy skillet. With the back of your hand, press pepper into steaks. Let stand 15 minutes. Sprinkle a large skillet over high heat with salt. When salt begins to brown, add oil and 3 teaspoons of the butter. Add steaks and cook 3 minutes. Turn with tongs and cook other side 3 minutes. Reduce heat to medium-low. Turn steaks and cook 3 to 5 minutes per side, depending on degree of desired doneness. In a small saucepan over low heat, melt remaining butter. Add Worcestershire sauce and lemon juice. Remove steaks from skillet. Cook drippings until almost evaporated. Return steaks to skillet. Pour butter mixture over steaks. Warm cognac in a small saucepan. Ignite with a kitchen match and pour over steaks. Transfer steaks to hot plates. Sprinkle steaks with chives or parsley. Place a spoonful of marmalade on the side of each plate, if desired. Makes 4 servings.

Sweet & Sour Meatballs

Serve over steamed rice or noodles.

1 pound lean ground beef
1/4 cup cooked long-grain rice
1 small onion, grated
1 egg, lightly beaten
1/8 teaspoon salt
1/8 teaspoon pepper
1 (6-oz.) can tomato paste
3/4 cup water
1/3 cup honey
1/4 cup raisins
1 tablespoon fresh lemon juice
1 lemon, thinly sliced

In a medium-size bowl, combine beef, rice, onion, egg, salt and pepper. Roll into small or mini-size balls. In a medium-size saucepan, combine tomato paste, water, honey, raisins, lemon juice and lemon slices. Gently add meatballs. Simmer over low heat 30 minutes. Remove lemon slices. Makes 2 or 3 servings.

Variations

Substitute ground or minced chicken or ground turkey for ground beef. Increase water to 1 cup.

Tip

Serve mini-size meatballs as an hors d'oeuvre. Pour sauce into a small bowl for dipping.

Lamb Ragoût

A hearty meal-in-one dish. Serve with a crusty loaf of bread.

2 pounds lean lamb, cut into 2-inch cubes
1/2 teaspoon salt
1/2 teaspoon pepper
1/4 cup vegetable oil
2 medium-size onions, coarsely chopped
1 to 2 garlic cloves, minced
1 to 2 cups beef broth or bouillon
5 tablespoons fresh lemon juice
2 tablespoons white-wine vinegar
1/4 teaspoon dried leaf tarragon
2 tablespoons butter
4 to 8 small potatoes
8 medium-size carrots, cut into 1-inch rounds
2 large green apples, peeled and quartered
1 cup frozen green peas
8 medium-size mushrooms, thickly sliced
2 tablespoons chopped fresh parsley

Preheat oven to 350°F (175°C). Season lamb with salt and pepper. In a Dutch oven, heat oil over medium heat and add lamb. Cook until browned on all sides. Remove with tongs or a slotted spoon. Add onions and garlic and sauté until transparent. Over low heat, stir in 1 cup of the broth, 2 tablespoons of the lemon juice, the vinegar and tarragon. Add browned meat, cover and roast 1-1/2 hours. Check ragoût occasionally while roasting and add remaining broth as needed. Meanwhile, in a large skillet over medium heat, melt butter. Add potatoes and cook until browned on all sides. Add carrots and apple quarters and sprinkle with 2 tablespoons of the lemon juice. Cover and simmer until potatoes are not quite tender, 20 to 25 minutes. Add to lamb after 1-1/4 hours. Add peas, mushrooms, carrots and apples the last 5 minutes of cooking. Transfer lamb and vegetables to a platter. Skim off fat, if any, from top of liquid. Adjust taste with remaining lemon juice. Spoon liquid over lamb and vegetables. Sprinkle with parsley. Makes 4 servings.

Broiled Marinated Lamb Chops

Rib chops have a very delicate flavor. Serve with a green salad and a baked potato.
It's great to eat chops at home; you can chew on the bones to your heart's content.

4 double lamb rib chops, 1-1/2 inches thick
Marinade, see below
Mint jelly (optional)

Marinade:
2 tablespoons extra-virgin olive oil
2 tablespoons fresh lemon juice
1 garlic clove, minced
1/2 teaspoon dried leaf tarragon
1/2 teaspoon dried leaf thyme
Salt
Freshly ground pepper

Place chops in a shallow dish. Prepare Marinade and pour over chops. Marinate at room temperature 1 hour, turning chops occasionally. Preheat broiler. Lightly oil broiler rack. Broil chops on rack 2 inches from heating element until browned on both sides, turning once and brushing with Marinade. Lower rack to 3 inches from heating element. Broil 8 to 10 minutes for medium-rare, 12 to 15 minutes for medium or 18 to 20 minutes for well done, turning and brushing with Marinade during cooking. Serve chops on very hot plates to prevent fat from congealing. Serve with mint jelly, if desired. Makes 2 to 4 servings.

Marinade

In a small bowl, combine all ingredients until well blended.

Tip

To insure a light delicate lamb flavor, buy young lamb, or what used to be called spring lamb, no more than six months old when butchered. The older the lamb the stronger the flavor.

Veal in Brandy Sauce

*Flaming this dish just before serving adds just
the right touch of drama and excitement to the meal.*

1 pound veal eye of round or veal cutlets
1/3 cup all-purpose flour
2 tablespoons butter or margarine
1/3 cup chopped shallots
6 tablespoons fresh lemon juice
6 tablespoons brandy
2 tablespoons chopped fresh parsley

If using veal eye of round, cut into 1/4-inch slices. Place veal between sheets of waxed paper. Using a meat tenderizer, pound veal until very thin. Dredge veal in flour. In a large skillet, melt butter over medium heat. Add the veal and sauté until lightly browned and cooked through, 1 to 2 minutes per side. Remove veal and keep warm. Add shallots to skillet and cook until softened, about 4 minutes. Return veal to the skillet. Increase heat to high. Add lemon juice and brandy. Carefully ignite with a kitchen match. Turn off heat. When flames have subsided, sprinkle with parsley. Makes 4 servings.

Veal Piccata

No lemon cookbook would be complete without a recipe for Veal Piccata. This one is as elegant and subtle as Veal Piccata should be.

1 pound veal eye of round or veal cutlets
1/2 cup all-purpose flour
1 tablespoon extra-virgin olive oil
1 tablespoon butter or margarine
1/4 cup white wine
2 tablespoons fresh lemon juice
2 tablespoons capers
Freshly ground pepper

If using veal eye of round, cut into 1/4-inch slices. Place veal between sheets of waxed paper. Using a meat tenderizer, pound veal until very thin. Dredge veal in flour. In a large skillet, heat oil and butter over high heat until very hot. Add the veal and sauté until lightly browned and cooked through, 1 to 2 minutes per side. Transfer the veal to a serving dish. Keep warm. Add the wine and lemon juice to the skillet. Bring to a boil, scraping up browned bits with a wooden spatula. Stir in capers and season with pepper. Pour over veal. Makes 4 servings.

Oven-fried Chicken

A great variation on the classic fried chicken without the extra calories.

1/4 cup butter or margarine, melted
1/4 cup fresh lemon juice
1 tablespoon grated lemon peel
1 cup Seasoned Bread Crumbs, see below
1 (2- to 3-lb.) chicken, cut into 8 pieces
4 lemon wedges

Seasoned Bread Crumbs:
4 to 6 slices egg or wheat bread, dried
1/2 teaspoon dried leaf oregano
1/2 teaspoon salt
1/4 teaspoon pepper

Preheat oven to 400°F (205°C). Place 2 cooling racks on a baking sheet that has a rim. The racks may overlap. In a shallow bowl, combine butter, lemon juice and lemon peel. Prepare Seasoned Bread Crumbs. Place crumbs in another shallow bowl. Dip chicken pieces into lemon mixture, then into bread crumbs, coating thoroughly. Place chicken on racks. Cover loosely with foil. Bake 45 minutes. Uncover and bake 20 minutes or until juices run clear when chicken is pierced with a fork. Serve with lemon wedges. Makes 4 servings.

Seasoned Bread Crumbs

Tear bread into large pieces and place in a blender. Process into crumbs. Add oregano, salt and pepper. Process to combine.

Baked Chicken with Dill

A great dish for the busy chef, as it can be prepared ahead of time. Serve with a bright green vegetable, yellow squash or grilled tomato and steamed rice or boiled potatoes.

1 (2- to 3-lb.) chicken, cut into 8 pieces, or 8
   chicken breast halves
Salt
Pepper
1/4 cup fresh lemon juice
1 teaspoon grated lemon peel
3 garlic cloves, minced
1 to 2 tablespoons chopped fresh dill
1 small onion, thinly sliced

Preheat oven to 350°F (175°C). Season chicken with salt and pepper. Place in a 13" x 9" baking dish. In a small bowl, combine lemon juice, lemon peel, garlic and dill. Using a pastry brush, coat chicken pieces with lemon juice mixture. Place onion slices on top. Cover pan with foil and bake 45 minutes. Uncover and bake 15 to 20 minutes or until lightly browned and juices run clear when chicken is pierced with a fork. Makes 4 servings.

Variation

Add 1 to 2 cups fresh or frozen green peas or green beans for the last 15 minutes of baking.

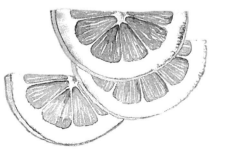

Whole Roasted Chicken with Rosemary

This chicken is as delicious as it is beautiful to serve.
It will bring back fond memories of past family dinners.

1 (3-lb.) roasting chicken
Salt
Pepper
1 tablespoon grated lemon peel
1 lemon, cut into 8 wedges
2 fresh rosemary sprigs or 2 teaspoons dried
  rosemary
4 carrots, cut into 1/2-inch slices
4 potatoes, peeled and cut into 2-inch slices
1 large onion, sliced
1 cup white wine
1/4 cup fresh lemon juice
1 tablespoon chopped fresh rosemary or 1
  teaspoon dried rosemary

Preheat oven to 375°F (190°C). Rub chicken, inside and out, with salt and pepper. Rub lemon peel over outside. Place lemon wedges and fresh rosemary sprigs inside cavity of chicken. Place chicken, breast side up, in a roasting pan. Arrange carrots, potatoes and onion around chicken. Pour wine and lemon juice over chicken and vegetables. Sprinkle with chopped rosemary. Bake 1-1/2 hours. Serve warm. Makes 4 servings.

Sautéed Chicken & Vegetables

Serve with lots of crusty bread to dip in the lemon sauce.

1 (3-lb.) chicken, cut into 8 pieces
Salt
Pepper
2 tablespoons vegetable oil
8 small red potatoes, scrubbed, unpeeled
    and halved
4 carrots, cut into 1/2-inch slices
1 large onion, chopped
3/4 pound frozen Brussels sprouts
1 bay leaf
2 tablespoons dried dill weed
3/4 cup chicken broth
1/4 cup fresh lemon juice
1 tablespoon chopped fresh parsley

Season chicken with salt and pepper. In a large Dutch oven, heat oil over medium heat. Add chicken and cook, turning until browned on all sides, 10 to 12 minutes. Add potatoes, carrots, onion, Brussels sprouts, bay leaf, dill, broth and lemon juice. Reduce heat to simmer. Cover and cook 40 minutes or until chicken and vegetables are tender. Remove chicken and vegetables to a serving platter. Spoon sauce over chicken and vegetables. Sprinkle with parsley. Makes 4 servings.

Tarragon Chicken with Mushrooms & Peas

You will savor every morsel of this tender chicken in its creamy sauce. Serve over noodles or rice with a side dish of carrots to add just the right color to the meal.

4 boneless skinless chicken breast halves
2 tablespoons butter or margarine
2 garlic cloves, minced
1 teaspoon grated lemon peel
3 cups mushrooms, quartered
2 tablespoons dry sherry
1 teaspoon dried leaf tarragon
Salt
Pepper
1-1/2 cups chicken broth
1-1/2 tablespoons fresh lemon juice
3 tablespoons all-purpose flour
3 tablespoons dairy sour cream
1 cup frozen green peas, thawed

Place chicken between sheets of waxed paper. Using a meat tenderizer, pound chicken until 1/4 inch thick. In a large skillet over medium heat, melt butter. Add garlic and lemon peel and sauté 1 minute. Add chicken, mushrooms, sherry and tarragon. Season with salt and pepper to taste. Cook, turning chicken once, 5 to 7 minutes or until chicken is no longer pink in center. Remove chicken and mushrooms. Keep warm. Whisk together broth, juice and flour. Add to skillet. Bring to a boil and cook, whisking constantly, until thickened. Reduce heat to simmer. Stir in sour cream. Do not let boil. Add peas, chicken and mushrooms. Heat through. Makes 4 servings.

Broiled Turkey Breast

Turkey is not just for holidays anymore. Serve
with a baked sweet potato or sautéed pineapple.

1/2 boneless turkey breast with skin
Marinade, see below
Parsley

Marinade:
1/4 cup fresh lemon juice
1/4 cup honey
1 teaspoon grated lemon peel
1 teaspoon sesame seeds
1/4 teaspoon ground sage
1/4 teaspoon dry mustard
1/8 teaspoon paprika
Salt
Pepper

Place turkey breast in a shallow dish. Prepare Marinade. Pour Marinade over turkey. Marinate in the refrigerator 1 to 1-1/2 hours, turning occasionally. Preheat broiler 10 minutes. Lightly oil broiler rack. Place turkey breast on broiler rack, skin-side down 8 inches from the broiler element. Broil 20 minutes. Turn turkey breast and place a meat thermometer in the thickest part of the breast. Move broiler rack 5 inches from element. Broil 15 to 20 minutes or until thermometer registers 190°F (90°C). Skin will blacken. Remove skin and discard. Slice turkey into thick slices. Place on a warm platter. In a small saucepan over low heat, simmer Marinade 10 minutes. Pour over turkey. Garnish with parsley. Makes 4 servings.

Marinade

In a small bowl, combine all ingredients. Cover and refrigerate 1 to 2 hours.

Vegetables & Rice

Vegetables are a great source of vitamins and minerals. They are low in calories and delicious when prepared with lemon. Special sauces and butters turn a simply prepared dish into a gourmet delight.

A rice dish can be the focal point of a simple dinner or a complement to a more elaborate dinner. Of course, all rice dishes are at their best when prepared with a touch of lemon.

TIPS FOR USING LEMONS WITH VEGETABLES

- Most vegetables that are boiled or steamed can be served with lemon butter, made with 1 pat melted butter to 1/4 to 1 teaspoon fresh lemon juice, depending on taste.
- Vegetables can be served with a squeeze of fresh lemon juice.
- To add extra zest to vegetables, spices and herbs can be added to lemon butter or lemon juice. Use herbs and spices sparingly at first, a dash to 1/8 teaspoon. Try herb and spice combinations.
- Listed below are vegetable, herb and spice combinations that blend well with lemon butter or fresh lemon juice:

  Basil—artichokes, broccoli, green beans, potatoes, spinach, green peas, squash and zucchini

  Caraway seeds—beets, broccoli, cabbage, carrots, cauliflower, green beans and spinach

  Dill—new potatoes

  Ginger—artichokes, broccoli, carrots, green beans, green peas, spinach and zucchini

  Marjoram—mushrooms and summer squash

  Mint—carrots and green peas

  Oregano—artichokes, spinach and squash

  Mustard—broccoli and cauliflower

  Rosemary—green peas, spinach and zucchini

  Sesame seeds—cauliflower, green peas and turnips

  Tarragon and thyme: asparagus, broccoli, Brussels sprouts, carrots and mushrooms

  Chervil, parsley and freshly ground pepper—almost all vegetables
- Serve sweeter vegetables, beets, carrots, green beans and green peas with lemon butter or fresh lemon juice combined with the following: cloves, freshly grated nutmeg or ground cinnamon. (You might want to balance cinnamon with sugar to taste.)
- Combine fresh lemon juice with sunflower kernels, pine nuts or poppy seeds.
- Be creative as you become more familiar with combining spices and herbs with lemon juice.

Artichokes with Lemon Dressing

A good source of potassium. Serve with a steak and baked potato for an All-American meal with just a touch of Italy.

4 small artichokes
2 to 3 tablespoons fresh lemon juice
3 tablespoons extra-virgin olive oil
1/2 teaspoon dried leaf basil
1 teaspoon poppy seeds
Salt
Pepper

Cut off bottom stems of artichokes. Cut off sharp points from leaves. In a medium-size saucepan, place artichokes in boiling salted water to cover. Boil, covered, about 45 minutes or until a leaf can be easily removed. Remove with a slotted spoon. Turn upside down to drain. Pat dry with paper towels. Keep warm until ready to serve. In a small bowl, beat juice, oil and basil with a wire whisk until blended. Add poppy seeds and season with salt and pepper to taste. Whisk dressing just before serving. Pour dressing into small glass bowls for easy dipping. Makes 4 servings.

Parsley-Lemon Rice

*A simple, but delicious, side dish that can
be served with baked fish or roasted turkey or chicken.*

2 tablespoons butter or margarine
1 small garlic clove
2 to 4 tablespoons fresh lemon juice
2 tablespoons chopped fresh parsley
1/4 teaspoon grated lemon peel
1 cup hot cooked rice

In a small skillet, melt butter. Add garlic and sauté until golden-brown. Discard garlic. Add lemon juice, parsley and lemon peel to butter and cook 1 minute. Pour over rice; toss until fluffy. Makes 2 servings.

Variations

Recipe can be doubled.

Lemon-Butter Rice: Omit parsley.

Peas & Wild Rice

Serve as either a side dish with meat or fish or make it the centerpiece of your vegetarian dinner. Serve with steamed carrots and fresh fruit.

1 cup wild rice
1 cup frozen green peas
1/4 to 1/2 cup salted, dry-roasted
   sunflower kernels
2 tablespoons butter or margarine, melted
2 to 4 tablespoons fresh lemon juice
1 teaspoon grated lemon peel

Follow package directions for steaming rice. Add peas and sunflower kernels to rice. Combine butter, 2 tablespoons of the lemon juice and the lemon peel. Pour over rice and toss gently. Cover and let stand several minutes. Add remaining lemon juice to taste. Makes 4 servings.

Variations

Substitute 1/2 cup white or brown rice for 1/2 cup wild rice or combine any of the three to make 1 cup of precooked rice. Substitute chopped dry-roasted and salted peanuts for sunflower kernels. Substitute toasted pine nuts for sunflower kernels. Add salt to taste.

Asparagus with Lemon Butter

Asparagus adds a gourmet touch to any main course.

1 pound medium-size asparagus
1/4 cup butter or margarine, melted
2 tablespoons fresh lemon juice
1 teaspoon grated lemon peel
Salt
Freshly ground pepper
2 tablespoons toasted slivered almonds

Cut white part off asparagus spears. Peel about 1/3 of stalk to discard tough outer skin. Remove small scales on stalk. Steam asparagus in an upright position until just tender. Do not overcook. Place in a heated serving dish. In a small saucepan over low heat, combine butter, lemon juice and lemon peel. Season with salt and pepper to taste. Cook, stirring, 1 minute or until heated. Sprinkle almonds over asparagus. Pour sauce over asparagus. Makes 4 servings.

Variations

Broccoli with Lemon Butter: Substitute 1 pound broccoli flowerets for asparagus.

Cauliflower with Lemon Butter: Substitute a medium-size cauliflower for asparagus. Cut into small flowerets. Substitute chopped cashews for almonds. Cook cashews in 1 teaspoon butter or margarine until lightly browned.

Steamed Beets

Beets make an attractive and delicious side dish.

1 tablespoon butter or margarine
1 tablespoon chopped fresh shallots or 1 teaspoon
    dried shallots
1 small garlic clove, finely chopped
1 teaspoon dried leaf tarragon
3/4 teaspoon caraway seeds
3 tablespoons fresh lemon juice
5 tablespoons water
12 small whole beets
Salt
Pepper

In a medium-size skillet over medium heat, melt butter. Add shallots, garlic, tarragon and caraway seeds; cook 2 to 3 minutes. Reduce heat to low. Add lemon juice, 3 tablespoons of the water and the beets. Cover skillet and steam beets until just tender, turning occasionally. Add remaining water as needed. Season with salt and pepper to taste. Makes 4 servings.

Sweet & Sour Red Cabbage

*Serve with a good pot roast for a hearty meal
on a winter night. Another good source of vitamin C.*

2 tablespoons butter or margarine
1/2 onion, finely chopped
1 small head red cabbage, shredded
1 large apple, peeled, grated
3/4 cup water
1/4 to 1/3 cup fresh lemon juice
1 to 2 tablespoons brown sugar
1 teaspoon salt
1 to 2 tablespoons all-purpose flour

In a large skillet, melt butter. Add onion and cook until tender. Add cabbage, apple and 1/2 cup of the water. Simmer, covered, over low heat 5 minutes, stirring occasionally. In a small saucepan over low heat, combine lemon juice, brown sugar, salt and remaining water. Stir in flour until smooth; cook 1 minute. Pour over cabbage. Cover and cook another 5 to 10 minutes until cabbage is just tender. Makes 6 servings.

Carrots with Lemon Glaze

*Lots of beta-carotene! Start with the smaller amounts
of brown sugar and lemon juice, and add more as needed.*

2 cups thinly sliced carrots
1 tablespoon butter or margarine
2 to 3 teaspoons brown sugar
2 to 3 teaspoons fresh lemon juice
1/8 teaspoon freshly grated nutmeg
1 teaspoon grated lemon peel

In a medium-size pan, steam carrots over boiling water until just tender. In a small skillet, melt butter; add sugar, lemon juice and nutmeg and cook, stirring constantly, 2 to 3 minutes. Place carrots in a warm serving dish. Pour juice mixture over carrots. Toss gently. Sprinkle with lemon peel. Makes 4 servings.

Cauliflower in Lemon Marinade

Serve as a side dish, in salads or on a relish tray.

1 medium-size cauliflower
Lemon Marinade, see below

Lemon Marinade:
3 to 4 tablespoons extra-virgin olive oil
2 to 3 tablespoons fresh lemon juice
1 teaspoon sesame seeds
1/2 teaspoon dry mustard
Salt
Freshly ground pepper

Cut cauliflower into small flowerets. In a medium-size pan, steam cauliflower until just tender, 3 to 5 minutes. Remove from pan and rinse with cold water. Prepare marinade and pour over cauliflower. Toss gently. Cover and refrigerate 3 hours, turning cauliflower occasionally. Makes 4 servings.

Lemon Marinade

In a small bowl, combine all ingredients.

Variation

Substitute 3/4 pound broccoli flowerets for cauliflower. Substitute caraway seeds for sesame seeds.

Broiled Marinated Mushrooms

Makes a quick tasty vegetable to complement broiled fish,
meat or chicken. Can be served as an appetizer or hors d'oeuvre.

12 large mushrooms
3/4 cup French Dressing (page 32)
Garlic Bread Crumbs, see below

Garlic Bread Crumbs:
2 bread slices, dried, torn into pieces
1 tablespoon Lemon Butter (page 76)
1 small garlic clove
2 tablespoons freshly grated Parmesan cheese

Marinate mushrooms in French Dressing in the refrigerator overnight. Preheat broiler. Remove mushrooms with a slotted spoon; discard dressing. Arrange on an ungreased broiler pan. Prepare Garlic Bread Crumbs. Sprinkle over mushrooms. Place pan 3 inches from heating element. Broil until crumbs turn light golden-brown, 4 to 7 minutes. Makes 4 servings.

Garlic Bread Crumbs

Add bread to a blender, process into crumbs. In a small skillet over medium heat, melt Lemon Butter. Add garlic; sauté until garlic is browned. Remove garlic. Remove skillet from heat, stir in bread crumbs. Cool slightly and stir in cheese.

Variations

Substitute either 1 pound broccoli or cauliflower flowerets, or 4 small scrubbed zucchini, scored with a fork and cut into 1/4-inch slices, for mushrooms.

New Potatoes

*Serve with broiled meat or fish. For a delicious vegetarian dinner, serve with
a grilled tomato and steamed broccoli.*

3 tablespoons extra-virgin olive oil
3 tablespoons chopped fresh dill or 1 tablespoon
  dried dill
1 tablespoon chopped fresh shallots or 1 teaspoon
  dried shallots
1 medium-size garlic clove, finely chopped
1/2 cup fresh lemon juice
1/4 cup water
1 teaspoon salt
1/4 teaspoon freshly ground pepper
8 small new potatoes, red or white, well scrubbed,
  unpeeled
Paprika

In a heavy skillet, heat oil over medium heat. Add dill, shallots and garlic; cook 1 minute. Stir in 1/4 cup of the lemon juice, the water, salt and pepper. Reduce heat to low and add potatoes. Turn potatoes so that they are evenly coated. Cover and cook until potatoes are tender, turning occasionally. Potato skins should become a little crusty and dark-brown in spots. Just before removing potatoes from skillet, spoon remaining lemon juice over each potato. Sprinkle with paprika. Makes 4 servings.

Variation

Substitute fresh or dried basil for dill.

Zucchini with Lemon Vinaigrette

Serve as a side dish with leftover beef roast, cold roasted
chicken or turkey, or as a salad arranged on lettuce leaves.

6 medium-size zucchini
1/2 cup extra-virgin olive oil
1/4 cup fresh lemon juice
2 medium-size garlic cloves, finely chopped
2 tablespoons finely chopped fresh parsley
1/2 teaspoon salt
Freshly ground pepper
1/4 cup toasted chopped cashews

Score zucchini with a fork in a vertical pattern. Slice zucchini into 1/4-inch rounds. In a medium-size pan, steam zucchini over boiling water 2 minutes. Remove from pan and rinse under cold water. Pat dry with paper towels. Place zucchini in a serving bowl. In a small bowl, combine olive oil, lemon juice, garlic, parsley, salt and pepper. Pour dressing over zucchini. Toss lightly. Refrigerate 1 hour, tossing zucchini several times. To serve, remove zucchini from dressing with a slotted spoon. Sprinkle cashews over zucchini. Makes 4 servings.

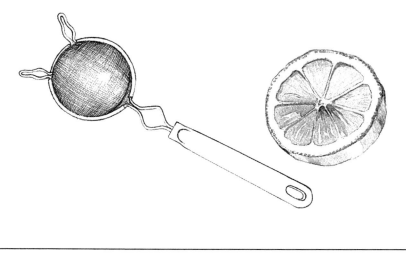

Lemon Butter

Place a pat over broiled fish, veal or chicken.

1/4 cup butter or margarine
1 teaspoon finely grated lemon peel
1 teaspoon fresh lemon juice

Cream butter and lemon peel until soft. Gradually stir in juice. Form into a log on plastic wrap, roll in wrap and refrigerate until chilled. Makes 4 pats or 1/4 cup.

Hollandaise Sauce

This simplified version of Hollandaise makes the plainest cooked vegetable a special dish. Serve over asparagus, broccoli or broiled fish.

1/2 cup butter
1-1/2 tablespoons fresh lemon juice
1/8 teaspoon salt
Pinch of red (cayenne) pepper
3 egg yolks, free of all whites

In a small saucepan, melt butter. Add juice, salt and cayenne. To a small double boiler over simmering water, add egg yolks, beating with a wire whisk until thick and foamy. Gradually add butter mixture, beating constantly until sauce has the consistency of mayonnaise. If sauce becomes too thick, whisk in a little boiling water. Makes 1/2 cup.

Tip

Separate an egg by letting the egg white drip through the fingers of your hand. All that will remain in your hand will be the yolk.

Béarnaise Sauce

This is a very rich sauce that uses Hollandaise Sauce as its base and adds herbs. Great for steamed, poached or grilled fish and grilled or sautéed meat.

1-1/2 tablespoons fresh lemon juice
1-1/2 tablespoons white-wine vinegar
2 tablespoons finely chopped shallots or
   green onion bulbs
1 teaspoon dried leaf tarragon
1 teaspoon dried leaf parsley
Hollandaise Sauce (see opposite page)
1/2 teaspoon dried leaf chervil
Dash of red (cayenne) pepper
Salt
Black pepper

In a small saucepan over medium-high heat, combine lemon juice, vinegar, shallots, tarragon and parsley. Cook until liquid is reduced to less than half. Prepare Hollandaise Sauce. Using a wire whisk, add reduced liquid to sauce and stir. Add chervil, cayenne, salt and black pepper. This sauce is better if prepared just before serving. If prepared in advance, it will keep in the top of a double boiler over warm water a few minutes. Makes 2/3 cup.

Lemon-Butter Sauce

Serve over broiled shellfish or fish.

1/4 cup butter or margarine
1 teaspoon fresh lemon juice
1 tablespoon chopped capers

In a small saucepan, melt butter. Stir in juice and capers. Pour over grilled or broiled fish. Makes 1/4 cup.

Breads, Cakes, Cookies & Pies

Breads baked with lemon have just the right hint of tartness. Try the following recipes and see what I mean.

The recipes in this book go from a very subtle lemon taste to a smack-in-the-mouth tartness, which should please all lemon lovers. I hope you have as much fun making and eating them as I have had developing and tasting them.

QUICK TIPS FOR SUCCESSFUL BAKED GOODS

- Read the recipe through completely. Assemble all ingredients.
- Measure all ingredients accurately. Level all dry ingredients with a knife. Measure liquid ingredients in a liquid measuring cup with a lip for easy pouring.
- Bring butter and eggs to room temperature, unless otherwise called for in recipe.
- Use unsalted butter or margarine. Salt is called for when needed in a recipe.
- Butter is preferred because butter's flavor and texture are hard to duplicate with margarine. But margarine can be used if you are on a low cholesterol diet. If you can, use butter in cookies.
- Use fresh ingredients. Nuts should be refrigerated or frozen to prevent rancidity. Spices and leavening agents such as baking powder and soda lose their effectiveness with age.
- Use pure extracts, not imitations.
- Stir or sift dry ingredients thoroughly, so that all leavening agents, salt and spices are evenly distributed.
- Preheat oven at least 10 minutes before baking. If you have an oven thermometer, use it.
- Know your own oven. All baking times given are to be used as a guide. Ovens vary in temperature accuracy. Altitude and different makes of pans affect temperature and baking times.
- It is easier to handle cookie or pie dough after refrigerating 30 minutes.
- When rolling pie or cookie dough, use a delicate touch and as little extra flour as possible.
- When using more than one baking sheet at a time, to ensure even baking, halfway through baking rotate positions of baking sheets, top to bottom, back to front. When using one baking sheet, turn sheet around halfway through baking.
- When testing cakes or breads for doneness, use the wooden pick or skewer method. Place wooden pick in center of cake or bread. If the wooden pick comes out clean, the cake or bread is done. (There are also thin wire cake testers that can be purchased inexpensively.)

Lemon Twist

This attractive bread tastes as good as it looks.

1 (1/4-oz.) package active dry yeast
1/2 cup plus 2 tablespoons warm water (115°F, 45°C)
5 eggs
1/3 cup sugar
1/2 cup butter or margarine, melted and cooled
2 teaspoons grated lemon peel
1 teaspoon salt
4 cups all-purpose flour
1 teaspoon baking soda
1 to 2 tablespoons lemon extract
1/2 cup raisins
1/4 cup coarsely chopped walnuts (optional)
1 tablespoon water
Walnut or pecan halves

In a large bowl, combine yeast and 2 tablespoons of the warm water. In a medium-size bowl, lightly beat 4 of the eggs. Stir in remaining warm water, sugar, melted butter, lemon peel and salt. Add to yeast mixture with 2 cups of the flour, 1 cup at a time. Mix until smooth. Stir in baking soda and lemon extract. Stir in remaining flour, or as much as is necessary to make a soft dough. Place on a floured board and knead 5 to 8 minutes. Work in additional flour as needed. Place dough in a greased bowl and turn lightly to coat. Cover loosely with plastic wrap and a dish towel and let rise in a warm area until dough doubles in size, about 1-1/2 hours. Punch dough down. On floured board, knead raisins and walnuts into dough, about 5 minutes. Cover and let stand 30 minutes. Preheat oven to 350°F (175°C). Spray a baking sheet with nonstick cooking spray. Divide dough into 3 pieces. Roll each piece into a rope, about 16 inches long. Loosely braid the 3 ropes together. Pinch ends and tuck under to secure. Place on prepared baking sheet. Cover and let rise 1 hour. Beat remaining egg and the 1 tablespoon water together. Brush evenly over bread. Decorate with walnut halves. Bake 25 to 30 minutes. Remove to a wire rack to cool. Makes 1 loaf.

Spiced Sweet Potato Bread

A hearty bread that combines several flavors—sweet, tart and spicy.

1/2 cup butter or margarine, room temperature
3/4 cup firmly packed brown sugar
2 eggs
3/4 cup mashed cooked sweet potato
1/2 cup plain yogurt
3 tablespoons fresh lemon juice
2 teaspoons grated lemon peel
1/2 cup chopped walnuts
3/4 cup golden raisins
2 cups sifted all-purpose flour
1 teaspoon baking powder
1 teaspoon baking soda
1/2 teaspoon salt
1/2 teaspoon ground cinnamon
1/4 teaspoon freshly grated nutmeg
1/4 teaspoon ground ginger
Lemon Glaze, see below

Lemon Glaze:
2 tablespoons fresh lemon juice
2 tablespoons butter, melted
3 tablespoons sugar
1 teaspoon grated lemon peel

Preheat oven to 375°F (190°C). Grease a 10-inch springform tube pan. In a large bowl, using an electric mixer, cream butter. Add sugar and beat until well blended. Beat in eggs, one at a time until blended. Stir in sweet potato. In a small bowl, combine yogurt, lemon juice, lemon peel, walnuts and raisins. Stir into egg mixture. Sift together flour, baking powder, soda, salt and spices. Add to egg mixture all at once. Stir with a wooden spoon until the dry ingredients are just blended, but mixture is still lumpy. Spoon into

pan. Smooth with a spatula. Bake 45 to 50 minutes or until a wooden pick inserted in center comes out clean. Remove from oven. Set oven to broil. Puncture bread with a fork in several places. Prepare glaze. Drizzle glaze over bread. Move rack to lowest position. Broil bread 2 to 3 minutes, until glaze bubbles. Watch bread to make sure it does not burn. Remove to wire rack to cool 15 minutes. Remove bread from pan and cool thoroughly. Makes 1 round loaf.

Lemon Glaze

In a small bowl, combine all ingredients.

Variation

Delete spices from flour mixture. Add spices to glaze.

Lemon Scones

Serve with strawberry jam, Lemon Curd (page 106) and whipped sweet butter.

2 T + 2 cups sifted all-purpose flour
2 tablespoons sugar
2 tablespoons grated lemon peel
4½ t. 2 tablespoons baking powder
1/2 teaspoon salt
1/2 cup butter, chilled
1 egg, slightly beaten
2/3 cup buttermilk, room temperature
2 T 1 teaspoon lemon extract *juice*
1/4 cup currants
1/4 cup chopped blanched almonds
Glaze, see below

Glaze:
1-1/2 tablespoons fresh lemon juice
1 tablespoon sugar

Preheat oven to 425°F (220°C). Lightly grease a baking sheet or spray with nonstick cooking spray. In a large bowl, combine flour, sugar, lemon peel, baking powder and salt. Using a pastry blender, cut butter into flour mixture until mixture is the texture of coarse meal. Add egg, 1/2 cup of the buttermilk and the lemon extract. Add remaining buttermilk, a tablespoon at a time, if needed, to make a soft dough. Turn the dough onto a lightly floured board and knead in currants and almonds. Divide dough in half. Shape each half into a smooth ball. Press out each ball with your hand to a 6-inch round. Cut each round into 4 to 8 wedges. Prepare Glaze. Brush Glaze evenly over scones. Place scones on prepared baking sheet 1 inch apart. Bake in top third of oven 15 minutes or until golden-brown. Remove from pan. Cool slightly on a wire rack. Serve warm. Reheat by placing scones on an oven rack at the lowest position under broiler 2 minutes. Makes 8 to 16 scones.

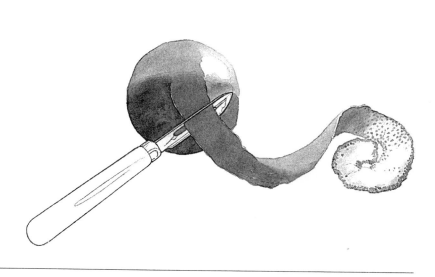

Glaze

In a very small saucepan, combine lemon juice and sugar. Simmer over low heat, stirring constantly, 2 minutes.

Variation

Substitute 2 cups whole-wheat flour for all-purpose flour. Decrease buttermilk by 1 tablespoon during first addition.

Lemon Bread

*Sure to become a favorite with the whole family. Delicious
served with a fresh fruit salad. Try it toasted for breakfast.*

1 egg
1 cup lemon marmalade
1 tablespoon butter, melted and cooled
2 cups sifted all-purpose flour
2 teaspoons baking powder
1/2 teaspoon baking soda
1/2 teaspoon salt
1/2 cup buttermilk
1 tablespoon fresh lemon juice
1/2 cup chopped walnuts

Preheat oven to 350°F (175°C). Grease an 8" x 4" loaf pan. In a large bowl, beat egg until thickened. Stir in marmalade and butter until well blended. Sift together flour, baking powder, soda and salt. Combine buttermilk and lemon juice. Alternately add dry and liquid ingredients in thirds to egg mixture, stirring until batter is mixed. Fold in chopped walnuts. Pour into loaf pan and bake 50 to 55 minutes or until a wooden pick inserted in center comes out clean. Let cool in pan about 5 minutes. Remove bread from pan. Cool thoroughly on a wire rack. Wrap loaf in foil. Makes 1 loaf.

Cheesecake

A light delicate cake—everyone's favorite.

Graham Cracker Crust, see below
4 eggs
1 cup sugar
1/4 cup fresh lemon juice
1 tablespoon grated lemon peel
1 teaspoon lemon extract or 1 teaspoon vanilla
  extract (optional)
4 cups cottage cheese
2 tablespoons all-purpose flour
1/8 teaspoon salt
3/4 cup whipping cream

Graham Cracker Crust:
15 graham crackers (1-1/2 cups)
3/4 cup plus 2 tablespoons butter or
  margarine, melted
1/4 cup plus 2 tablespoons powdered
  sugar, sifted
1-1/2 teaspoons grated lemon peel

Preheat oven to 300°F (150°C). Prepare Graham Cracker Crust mixture, and reserve 1/2 cup of crust mixture. Press remaining crumbs on the bottom of a 10-inch springform pan with the back of your hand. Refrigerate until thoroughly chilled. In a large bowl, beat eggs. Gradually beat in sugar. Add lemon juice, lemon peel and lemon extract, if using. In a blender, blend cottage cheese, flour and salt until smooth and creamy. In a small bowl, whip cream until soft peaks form. Fold cottage cheese and cream into egg mixture. Pour into the springform pan. Sprinkle the remaining graham cracker crumbs over middle of the cake. Bake 1 hour. Turn off heat and open oven door. Leave cake in the oven 30 minutes to 1 hour, until cool. Gently remove cake from pan. Refrigerate. Makes 10 servings.

Graham Cracker Crust

Grind crackers in a blender into very fine crumbs. In a medium-size bowl, combine crumbs, butter, sugar and lemon peel until combined.

Lemon Layer Cake

A lemon lover's cake.

1/2 cup plus 2 tablespoons butter or margarine,
  room temperature
1-1/2 cups sugar
2 eggs, lightly beaten
2 teaspoons lemon extract
1 teaspoon grated lemon peel
2 cups sifted cake flour
2 teaspoons baking powder
1/4 teaspoon baking soda
1/8 teaspoon salt
3/4 cup milk
Lemon Butter Filling, see below
Lemon Icing, see below
Shaved chocolate (optional)

Lemon Butter Filling:
1/4 cup butter, room temperature
2/3 cup powdered sugar, sifted
1 tablespoon fresh lemon juice

Lemon Icing:
1-3/4 cups powdered sugar, sifted
2 teaspoons grated lemon peel
1/3 cup butter or margarine, room temperature
3 to 4 tablespoons boiling water
1 teaspoon lemon extract

Preheat oven to 350°F (175°C). Grease and lightly flour 2 (9-inch) round cake pans. Line the bottom of each pan with parchment paper. Grease paper. In a large bowl, using an electric mixer, cream butter.

Gradually beat in sugar until well blended. Beat in eggs. Add lemon extract and lemon peel. In a small bowl, sift together flour, baking powder, soda and salt. Add the dry ingredients to the butter mixture in 3 parts, alternating with milk. Stir batter after each addition. Pour batter into prepared pans and bake 20 to 25 minutes or until cakes pull away from sides of pans. Cool on a wire rack 5 minutes. Remove cakes from pans and peel paper off bottoms. Cool thoroughly. Turn one layer onto a cake plate, bottom side up. Cover exposed parts of plate with strips of waxed paper to protect plate from drippings. Prepare Lemon Butter Filling. Spread filling on top of layer. Cover with remaining cake, bottom side down. Prepare Lemon Icing. Frost cake with icing, spreading on top and sides of cake with a spatula. Decorate with shaved chocolate, if using. When icing is set, 5 to 10 minutes, remove waxed paper from plate. Makes 10 to 12 servings.

Lemon Butter Filling

In a small bowl, cream butter. Gradually add sugar to butter until well blended. Add lemon juice and beat 5 minutes.

Lemon Icing

Combine sugar and lemon peel in the top of a double boiler. Fill the bottom half with hot, not boiling, water, add top and let stand 1 hour, or until water cools. In a medium-size bowl, using an electric mixer, cream butter. Add sugar; beat until blended, gradually stirring in just enough water to make a thin spreadable icing. Add lemon extract. Beat 5 minutes.

Variation

Lemon-Cocoa Filling: Add 1/4 cup unsweetened cocoa powder to powdered sugar in the filling on the opposite page before sifting.

Tip

After spreading frosting, dip spatula in hot water, then use to smooth top and sides of cake. Swirl frosting in center of cake.

Lemon Sponge Cake

One of my personal favorite desserts. Lemon Sauce can also be served on pancakes, waffles and French toast.

6 egg yolks
1 cup sugar
1 tablespoon fresh lemon juice
1 teaspoon grated lemon peel
1 cup sifted cake flour
1-1/2 teaspoons baking powder
1/4 teaspoon salt
6 egg whites
Powdered sugar
Lemon Sauce, see below
1-1/2 cups strawberries or blueberries
1/2 cup whipping cream, whipped

Lemon Sauce:
1/2 cup sugar
1 tablespoon cornstarch
1/2 cup water
1/4 cup fresh lemon juice
1/2 teaspoon vanilla extract
1/4 teaspoon ground ginger

Preheat oven to 325°F (165°C). Grease a 10-inch tube pan and lightly flour the bottom. In a large bowl, using an electric mixer, beat egg yolks until thickened. Gradually beat in sugar until well blended. Add lemon juice and lemon peel. In a small bowl, sift together flour, baking powder and salt. Add the dry ingredients to egg mixture. Stir until well blended. In a medium-size bowl, beat egg whites until soft peaks form. Fold lightly into batter. Pour batter into pan and bake 45 to 50 minutes or until cake springs back when pressed in center. Invert the cake pan until cool. Remove cake from pan. Place cake on a serving plate. Sift powdered sugar over top of cake. Prepare Lemon Sauce. In separate bowls, arrange sauce, berries and whipped cream for toppings. Pass bowls with cake. Makes 10 to 12 servings.

Lemon Sauce

In a small saucepan over medium heat, combine sugar and cornstarch. Stir in water; cook, stirring constantly, until mixture thickens. Remove from heat. Stir in lemon juice, vanilla and ginger. Return to heat, stirring until syrupy, about 2 minutes. Serve hot. Can be reheated. Makes 3/4 cup.

Lemon-Filled Sandwich Cookies

Alternate this cookie with a chocolate cookie for a delightful combination of tastes.

1 cup butter or margarine, room temperature
1-1/4 cups sugar
2 eggs
2 teaspoons grated lemon peel
3 cups sifted all-purpose flour
1/4 teaspoon salt
1 cup Lemon Curd (page 106) or 1 cup Lemon
   Butter Filling (page 88)

Preheat oven to 350°F (175°C). In a large bowl, using an electric mixer, cream butter. Gradually add sugar. Beat until well blended. Beat in eggs and lemon peel. In a medium-size bowl, sift together flour and salt. Add flour and salt to butter mixture; mix into a soft dough. Refrigerate several hours for easier handling. Divide dough in half. Roll each portion 1/8 inch thick on a lightly floured board. Cut into 2-inch rounds. Transfer rounds to an ungreased baking sheet, 1 inch apart. If cookies stick to board, lift with a small metal spatula and add more flour to board. Repeat until all dough is used. Bake 8 to 10 minutes or until edges are lightly browned. Transfer cookies to a wire rack to cool. Prepare Lemon Curd or Lemon Butter Filling. Turn half of the cookies over. Spread curd or filling on bottoms. Gently cover with the remaining cookies. Makes 40 sandwich cookies.

Nut Squares with Lemon Glaze

A delicious light and moist treat that is perfect for breakfast, brunch or afternoon tea.

2 eggs
1/3 cup butter or margarine, melted and cooled
3/4 cup honey
1/4 cup buttermilk
1 tablespoon fresh lemon juice
1 to 2 tablespoons grated lemon peel
1-1/2 cups sifted all-purpose flour
1 teaspoon baking powder
1/2 teaspoon baking soda
1 teaspoon salt
1/2 cup chopped walnuts
Lemon Glaze, see below

Lemon Glaze:
3 tablespoons honey
3 tablespoons fresh lemon juice
1 tablespoon grated lemon peel

Preheat oven to 350°F (175°C). Grease an 8-inch-square cake pan. In a large bowl, beat eggs until light. Add butter, honey, buttermilk, lemon juice and lemon peel. Stir until well blended. In a small bowl, sift together flour, baking powder, soda and salt. Add to egg mixture; stir until combined. Fold in walnuts. Pour into prepared pan and bake 30 to 35 minutes or until cake pulls away from sides of pan. While cake is baking, prepare glaze. Cool cake in pan 5 minutes. Turn out cake onto a wire rack, bottom side up. With a wooden pick, puncture cake 10 to 15 times. Drizzle half of the glaze over the cake. Turn cake over and repeat with remaining glaze. Cool on rack 5 minutes. Cut into squares. Serve warm or at room temperature. Makes 16 squares.

Lemon Glaze

In a small bowl, combine all ingredients.

Chocolate Surprise

A mystery cookie that will delight both lovers of chocolate and lemon.

1 cup butter, room temperature
3/4 cup sugar
1 egg
3 tablespoons lemon extract
2 cups sifted all-purpose flour
1/4 teaspoon salt
1/2 cup finely ground almonds
1 teaspoon grated lemon peel
36 chocolate kisses
1 cup coarsely chopped almonds

Preheat oven 325°F (165°C). In a large bowl, using an electric mixer, cream butter. Gradually add sugar and beat until well blended. Add egg and lemon extract and beat until mixture is light and creamy. In a small bowl, sift together flour and salt. Stir in ground almonds and lemon peel. Using a wooden spoon, add dry ingredients to egg mixture; stir until blended. Do not overmix. This is a very soft dough. Refrigerate 1 hour for easier handling. Roll dough into 1-1/2-inch balls around a chocolate kiss, covering kiss completely. Roll each ball in chopped almonds. Place on an ungreased baking sheet 1 inch apart. Bake in upper third of oven 12 to 15 minutes or until cookie just begins to brown around the edges. Remove from pan. Cool on a wire rack. Makes 36 cookies.

Variations

Lemon Rounds: Delete chocolate kisses. Roll dough in solid balls and complete according to above instructions. Prepare Chocolate Topping (page 94). Dip each cookie top in topping . Makes 24 cookies.

Cocoa-Lemon Rounds: Add 1/4 cup unsweetened cocoa powder to flour. Delete chocolate kisses.

Cream-Filled Meringue Cookies

This is a delicate flourless cookie. Crunchy to taste and attractive to look at.

1/4 cup powdered sugar, sifted
1/2 teaspoon grated lemon peel
2 egg whites
1/8 teaspoon cream of tartar
1 teaspoon lemon extract
1/2 cup finely ground walnuts
Chocolate Topping, see below
Lemon Curd (page 106)
Lemon Butter Filling (page 88) or Lemon-Cocoa
    Filling (page 89)

Chocolate Topping:
2 tablespoons chocolate chips
1 tablespoon milk
1/2 teaspoon vanilla extract

Preheat oven to 375°F (190°C). Line a large baking sheet with foil. Combine sugar and lemon peel. Beat egg whites until foamy. Add cream of tartar. Beat until soft peaks form. Gradually beat in sugar mixture; beat until stiff but not dry. Add lemon extract. Fold in ground walnuts. With a teaspoon, drop rounded spoonfuls 1 inch apart on baking sheet. Place baking sheet in upper half of oven and bake 1 minute. Turn off oven. Leave in oven 4 to 6 hours without opening oven door. Peel cookies from foil. Prepare Chocolate Topping. On half of the cookies, drizzle Chocolate Topping over the tops. Let dry 30 minutes. Prepare Lemon Curd or Lemon Butter Filling. Turn remaining cookies over. Spread with Lemon Curd or Lemon Butter Filling. Place a chocolate-topped cookie gently on top of a lemon-filled cookie. Makes 15 sandwich cookies.

Chocolate Topping
Combine chips and milk in the top of a double boiler over boiling water. This should be enough heat to melt chocolate chips. Stir in vanilla when chips have melted.

Lemon Thins

These thin cookies are rich in flavor. Divide
recipe and make several variations at one time.

1 cup butter or margarine, room temperature
1 cup sifted powdered sugar
1/4 cup fresh lemon juice
1 teaspoon grated lemon peel
1 teaspoon lemon extract or vanilla extract
2 cups sifted all-purpose flour
1/4 teaspoon salt

Preheat oven to 350°F (175°C). In a large bowl, using an electric mixer, cream butter. Gradually beat in sugar until well blended. Add lemon juice, lemon peel and lemon extract. In a small bowl, combine flour and salt. Gradually stir into butter mixture until well blended. Refrigerate dough until chilled for easy handling. Roll dough into 1-inch balls. Place balls 2-1/4 inches apart on an ungreased baking sheet. Dip a small spatula in hot water and use to press cookie balls flat until 2-1/2-inch-round cookies are formed. Bake 8 to 10 minutes, until sides of cookies just begin to turn a light golden-brown. Remove from baking sheet and cool on a wire rack. Makes 40 cookies.

Variations

Almond-Lemon Thins: Substitute 1 teaspoon almond extract for lemon extract. Decorate center of each cookie with one whole blanched almond.

Walnut-Lemon Thins: Combine 3/4 cup finely ground walnuts with sifted flour and salt. Decorate center of each cookie with a chopped walnut.

Chocolate-Lemon Thins: Stir 3/4 cup chocolate chips into cookie dough. Flatten to 2-inch cookies due to chips.

Lemon Thin Sandwiches: Using Lemon Butter Filling (page 88), follow directions for filling Lemon-Filled Sandwich Cookies (page 91).

Sand Tarts

An old-fashioned cookie with a lemon twist.

1/2 cup butter, room temperature
3/4 cup plus 1 tablespoon firmly packed
   brown sugar
1 egg
1 teaspoon lemon extract
2 teaspoons grated lemon peel
1-3/4 cups sifted all-purpose flour
1/8 teaspoon salt
2 teaspoons honey
1-1/2 tablespoons fresh lemon juice
48 blanched raw almonds (optional)

Preheat oven to 350°F (175°C). In a large bowl, using an electric mixer, cream butter. Gradually add brown sugar; mix until well blended. Beat in egg, lemon extract and 1-1/2 teaspoons of the lemon peel. Stir flour and salt into butter mixture and mix into a soft dough. Refrigerate several hours for easier handling. Divide dough in half. Roll each portion 1/8 inch thick on a lightly floured board or between 2 sheets of waxed paper. Cut into 2-inch rounds. Transfer rounds to an ungreased baking sheet 1 inch apart. If cookies stick to board, lift with a small metal spatula and add more flour to board. Repeat until all dough is used. Combine honey, lemon juice and remaining lemon peel. Brush over cookies. Top with an almond, if using. Bake 8 to 10 minutes or until edges turn a light golden-brown. Transfer cookies to a wire rack to cool. Makes 48 cookies.

Lemon Tarts

So rich that a little is enough.

Crème Fraîche, see below
1/2 cup butter or margarine, chilled
1 cup all-purpose flour
1 teaspoon sugar
1 teaspoon grated lemon peel
3 tablespoons plain yogurt
2 cups Lemon Curd (page 106)

Crème Fraîche:
1 cup whipping cream
1 tablespoon buttermilk
1 to 2 teaspoons grated lemon peel

Prepare Crème Fraîche ahead. Preheat oven to 450°F (230°C). In a medium-size bowl, using a pastry blender, cut butter into small chunks. Combine flour, sugar and lemon peel. Add dry ingredients to butter, and blend until mixture resembles coarse meal. Add yogurt 1 tablespoon at a time. Stir until blended. Using your hands, work together into a soft dough. Refrigerate several hours. Divide dough into 2 balls. On a lightly floured board, press each ball with back of your hand to form 5-inch rounds. Roll each ball to less than 1/8 inch thickness. Cut pastry into 4-inch rounds and fit over inverted muffin cups one cup apart, or line tart shells. Press sides and top firmly against forms. Prick with a fork and bake 10 minutes or until golden-brown. Turn halfway through baking to ensure even color. Cool 5 minutes. Remove and cool thoroughly on a wire rack. Prepare Lemon Curd. Fill each shell with 1/4 cup Lemon Curd. Serve tarts with Crème Fraîche. Makes 8 tarts.

Crème Fraîche

Pour cream into a small bowl, add buttermilk and lemon peel. Cover with plastic wrap and let stand in a warm place overnight. The consistency of the Crème Fraîche should be twice as thick as the cream was. To serve, pour into a small gravy boat. Makes 1 cup.

Lemon Meringue Pie

Brings back memories of Grandma—still a favorite today.

1 cup sugar
1/4 cup cornstarch
1/4 teaspoon salt
1 cup water
3 egg yolks, well beaten
1/2 to 2/3 cup fresh lemon juice
1 to 2 teaspoons grated lemon peel
1 tablespoon butter or margarine
1 baked 9-inch pie shell or 1 Graham Cracker
   Crust (page 87)
Meringue, see below

Meringue:
3 egg whites, room temperature
1 teaspoon vanilla extract
1/4 teaspoon cream of tartar
1/2 cup plus 1 tablespoon sifted powdered sugar

Preheat oven to 350°F (175°C). In a small saucepan over low heat, using a wire whisk, combine sugar, cornstarch and salt. Gradually stir in water. Add egg yolks, stirring constantly. Bring to a boil over medium heat; boil 1 minute. Remove from heat and stir in lemon juice, lemon peel and butter. Return to low heat and stir until mixture thickens. Pour filling into pie shell. Prepare Meringue. Spread Meringue on cooled pie filling, sealing outer edges first. Using a spatula, cover center of the pie with Meringue, making sure pie is completely sealed. Bake on lower third of oven 8 to 12 minutes or until Meringue is a light golden-brown. Makes 6 to 8 servings.

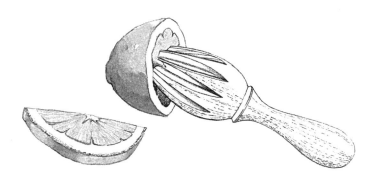

Meringue

In a large bowl, using an electric mixer, beat egg whites until foamy. Add vanilla and cream of tartar and beat until whites form soft peaks. Add sugar gradually and continue beating until stiff but not dry. Do not overbeat.

Variation

Mile-High Meringue: Use 5 egg whites, 1 teaspoon vanilla extract, 1/2 teaspoon cream of tartar, 1 cup sifted powdered sugar and follow directions above.

Tip

Ready-prepared pie crusts can be substituted for homemade crust.

Desserts & Beverages

Start your summer parties off with a cool refreshing lemon drink or your afternoon tea with Sparkling Lemon Punch (page 114) and Hot Spiced Lemonade (page 113). Also perfect for afternoon tea would be the Lemon Curd (page 106) spread on scones or cake.

Serve one of the classic lemon desserts such as Baked Lemon Soufflé (page 109) or Lemon Ice Cream (page 110) for a refreshing end to a meal.

Bread Pudding with Lemon Sauce

*Perfect on a cold winter's night. Great for breakfast served
with a tall glass of fresh orange juice and your favorite coffee.*

2-1/4 cups cubed day-old egg bread or leftover
  yellow cake or a combination
1-1/2 cups milk
1 egg
1/4 cup sugar
1 teaspoon lemon extract
1/2 teaspoon ground cinnamon
1/4 teaspoon grated nutmeg
2 tablespoons raisins or chopped dates
2 tablespoons pecans, toasted
1 teaspoon grated lemon peel
Lemon Sauce, see below
1/4 cup whipping cream (optional), whipped

Lemon Sauce:
1/4 cup sugar
1 teaspoon cornstarch
1/3 cup water
1 tablespoon butter
2 to 3 tablespoons fresh lemon juice
1/2 teaspoon grated lemon peel

Preheat oven to 325°F (165°C). Spray an 8-inch-square pan with nonstick cooking spray. Soak bread cubes in 1/2 cup of the milk. In a medium-size bowl, combine egg, sugar, lemon extract, cinnamon and nutmeg. Beat well. Beat in remaining milk. Stir in raisins, pecans and lemon peel. Combine egg mixture with bread. Pour pudding into prepared pan set in a larger pan. Add enough hot water to come halfway up sides of pan. Bake 40 to 50 minutes or until pudding is set in center. Prepare Lemon Sauce. Top each serving with Lemon Sauce and a spoonful of whipped cream, if using. Makes 4 servings.

Lemon Sauce

In a small saucepan over low heat, combine sugar and cornstarch. Using a wire whisk, gradually whisk in water and continue stirring until mixture thickens. Remove from heat and whisk in butter, lemon juice and lemon peel.

Tip

Lemon Sauce can be used over other desserts, ice creams, fruits and cakes.

Dried Fruit Compote

An old-fashioned dish. Serve as a side dish with pot roast,
roasted turkey or as a dessert with whipped cream or ice cream.

2 pounds assorted dried fruits
1 lemon, thinly sliced
2 to 3 cups apple juice
1-1/4 to 1-1/2 cups sugar
1/2 cup fresh lemon juice
1/4 cup fruit liqueur

In a medium-size saucepan, soak dried fruit and lemon slices in apple juice overnight. In a small bowl, combine sugar and lemon juice. Add to fruit and simmer over low heat until fruit is tender, 10 minutes. Remove from heat. Stir in liqueur. Serve warm or cold either in individual dessert dishes or in a glass serving bowl. Makes 8 servings.

Lemon Pudding Cake

Just as the name suggests, this dessert is a pudding with a cake topping.

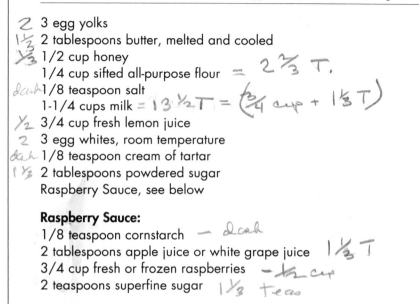

2   3 egg yolks
1½   2 tablespoons butter, melted and cooled
⅓   1/2 cup honey
     1/4 cup sifted all-purpose flour   = 2⅔ T.
dash 1/8 teaspoon salt
     1-1/4 cups milk = 13½ T = (¾ cup + 1⅓ T)
½   3/4 cup fresh lemon juice
2   3 egg whites, room temperature
dash 1/8 teaspoon cream of tartar
1⅓   2 tablespoons powdered sugar
     Raspberry Sauce, see below

Raspberry Sauce:
1/8 teaspoon cornstarch   — dash
2 tablespoons apple juice or white grape juice   1⅓ T
3/4 cup fresh or frozen raspberries   — ½ cup
2 teaspoons superfine sugar   1⅓ teas

Preheat oven to 350°F (175°C). Lightly grease 6 custard cups. In a medium-size bowl, using an electric mixer, beat egg yolks until thick and lemon-colored. Beat in butter and honey. Sift together flour and salt. Add to egg mixture and blend. Stir in milk and lemon juice. In a medium-size bowl, beat egg whites until foamy. Add cream of tartar and beat whites until soft peaks form. Gradually add 1-3/4 tablespoons of the powdered sugar. Beat until stiff but not dry. Do not overbeat. Fold into lemon mixture. Spoon into custard cups. Place cups in a baking dish with 1 inch hot water. Bake until pudding is set, about 30 to 35 minutes. Cool on a wire rack. Sift remaining powdered sugar over pudding. Serve warm or chilled. Prepare Raspberry Sauce. Top with Raspberry Sauce. Makes 6 cups.

Raspberry Sauce

In a small bowl, dissolve cornstarch in juice. In a small saucepan, combine all ingredients, and simmer 2 minutes, stirring, until thickened. Place in a blender and blend until smooth. Strain sauce. Add additional sugar to taste, if needed. Refrigerate until ready to use. Makes 1/2 cup.

Lemon Curd

Lemon Curd is a classic English lemon butter. Use as a spread on
English biscuits (cookies), as a filling for cakes or as a dessert.

1/2 cup butter
1/2 cup sugar or 1/3 cup honey
4 eggs plus 1 yolk, lightly beaten
1/2 cup fresh lemon juice
3 tablespoons grated lemon peel

Melt butter in a double boiler over simmering water. Add sugar; stir until dissolved. Using a wire whisk, beat in eggs, egg yolk, lemon juice and lemon peel. Cook over low heat, stirring with a wooden spoon, until mixture thickens. Do not overcook, as the curd may curdle and separate. Remove from hot water. Cool 5 minutes. Pour into containers and seal. Refrigerate up to 2 weeks. Makes 1-3/4 cups.

Variation

To serve as a dessert, pour into individual bowls. Refrigerate until chilled. Top with whipped cream and a mint sprig or a maraschino cherry.

Tip

Recipe can be halved if using only as a spread.

Lemon Mousse

A great dessert that can be made the day before.

1/2 cup butter or margarine
1 cup plus 1 tablespoon sugar
1/3 cup fresh lemon juice
2 teaspoons lemon peel
1/4 teaspoon salt
3 egg yolks, lightly beaten
3 egg whites
1 cup whipping cream
1/2 cup vanilla or chocolate cookie crumbs

In the top of a double boiler over simmering water, melt butter. Add 1 cup of the sugar and stir until sugar is dissolved. Add lemon juice, lemon peel and salt. Using a wire whisk, beat in yolks and stir 2 minutes. Cover and simmer 5 to 10 minutes or until mixture thickens, stirring occasionally. Cool. Pour into a large bowl. In another bowl, beat egg whites until foamy. Gradually add remaining 1 tablespoon sugar and beat until soft peaks form. Fold into custard. In a medium-size bowl, whip cream. Fold into custard. Pour gently into a 5-inch springform pan. Cover top with plastic wrap and foil. Freeze overnight. Refrigerate 2-1/2 hours before serving. Take out of refrigerator 30 minutes before serving. Place on a serving plate. Release spring and remove side of pan, leaving bottom on plate. Sprinkle top with cookie crumbs. Makes 4 to 5 servings.

Lemon Sorbet

Sorbet makes a refreshing dessert on a hot summer's eve. Serve with a simple cookie.
For a very elegant dinner, serve between courses, to clear the palate.

1 tablespoon grated lemon peel
2-1/4 cups water
3/4 cup sugar
1 cup fresh lemon juice

In a small saucepan, simmer peel in 1 cup of the water and the sugar 15 minutes. Cool. In a medium-size bowl, mix sugar syrup, juice and remaining water. Cover and place in freezer until semi-frozen. Pour into ice cream maker. Follow manufacturer's directions to freeze. Makes 6 servings.

Variation

Refrigerator Method: Pour sorbet mixture into ice trays. Cover and place in freezer until semi-frozen. Process in a blender until smooth and creamy. Return to trays and freeze until firm.

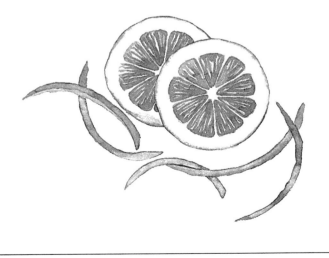

Baked Lemon Soufflé

*The aroma of a lemon soufflé served directly from oven to
table will be remembered long after this delicious dessert is eaten.*

5 egg yolks, room temperature
1/2 cup superfine sugar
1/4 cup fresh lemon juice
1-1/2 teaspoons grated lemon peel
2 tablespoons all-purpose flour
2 tablespoons butter or margarine, melted
1/2 cup milk, heated
6 egg whites, room temperature
1/4 teaspoon cream of tartar
1 teaspoon powdered sugar
1 cup whipping cream

Preheat oven to 350°F (175°C). Butter an 8-inch soufflé dish and lightly coat with powdered sugar. In a large bowl, beat egg yolks until thickened. Gradually beat in 1/4 cup of the superfine sugar until well blended. Add lemon juice and lemon peel. In a small saucepan over low heat, blend flour and butter. Stir in milk and cook, stirring constantly, until mixture is smooth and thickened. Remove from heat. Let cool 2 minutes. Stir into egg mixture. This process can be done an hour or so in advance, before proceeding to the final step. About 45 minutes before serving, so that soufflé can be served from oven to table, beat egg whites until foamy. Add cream of tartar. Gradually add remaining sugar and beat until soft peaks form. Mix 1/4 of the whites gently into the egg yolk mixture with a spatula. Gently fold the remaining egg whites into mixture. Place dish in a pan of hot, not boiling water, centering dish in lower half of oven. Bake 30 to 35 minutes or until firm. Sprinkle powdered sugar over soufflé and return to oven 2 to 3 minutes. Whip cream until soft peaks form. Serve with cream. Makes 6 servings.

Variation

Individual Soufflés: Pour soufflé mixture into 6 to 8 individual soufflé dishes or custard cups.

Lemon Ice Cream

Very creamy and refreshing with just the right amount of lemon flavor.

3 cups milk
1-1/2 cups sugar
1 tablespoon cornstarch
2 egg yolks
1 cup whipping cream
1 (6-oz.) can evaporated milk
6 tablespoons fresh lemon juice

In a medium-size saucepan, combine milk, sugar and cornstarch. Cook over medium heat, stirring frequently. When mixture begins to simmer, reduce heat to low. In a small bowl, beat egg yolks. Add about 1 cup of the hot mixture to the yolks, blending well. Return yolk mixture to saucepan. Cook, stirring, 2 minutes or until mixture is slightly thickened. Remove from heat. Stir in whipping cream, evaporated milk and lemon juice. Cool to room temperature. Freeze in an ice cream maker according to manufacturer's directions. Makes 2 quarts.

Lemonade

A classic recipe for the refreshing summer drink.

1-1/2 cups fresh lemon juice
1 cup sugar
8 cups cold water
Ice cubes
1 lemon, thinly sliced

Strain fresh lemon juice into a cold pitcher. Add sugar and 1/2 cup of the water, stirring until sugar dissolves. Stir in remaining water and ice cubes. Save 4 of the lemon slices for decoration. Float remaining slices in pitcher. Pour lemonade into large ice-filled glasses. Cut reserved lemon slices in half and place in each glass for decoration. Makes 8 servings.

Variations

Sparkling Lemonade: Substitute sparkling water for cold water for a little extra zing.

Honey Lemonade: Substitute 1/2 to 3/4 cup honey for sugar. Because honey is sweeter than sugar, adjust amount to taste.

Low-Calorie Lemonade: Substitute a low-calorie sweetener for sugar. Follow package's recommended equivalent amount.

Pink Lemonade: Add a few drops of red food coloring. Substitute several maraschino cherries for lemon slices. Top glass with a cherry. (For a special treat, delete food coloring and add 1/4 cup cherry liqueur. Adjust sugar.)

Orange Lemonade: Substitute 3/4 cup orange juice for 3/4 cup lemon juice. Reduce sugar to 3/4 cup. Float lemon and orange slices on top. Decorate glasses with either a halved lemon slice or a quartered orange slice.

Cinnamon Lemonade: Add 1/2 teaspoon ground cinnamon. Adjust sugar to taste. Decorate with a cinnamon stick in each glass.

Lemonade Syrup

Lemonade Syrup is useful for large parties or for your children's lemonade stand.

4-1/2 cups sugar
2 cups water
1/4 cup grated lemon peel
4-1/2 cups fresh lemon juice

In a medium-size saucepan, combine sugar, water and lemon peel. Boil liquid on medium to high heat, stirring constantly until liquid becomes syrupy. Strain. Cool. Add lemon juice. Pour into a sealed container and refrigerate until used. Makes 6 cups.

Variations

Classic Lemonade: Use 2 to 3 tablespoons Lemonade Syrup for each cup of water. Stir lemon syrup, water and ice cubes in a cold pitcher. Float lemon slices or mint sprigs on top. Decorate each glass with a lemon wedge or mint sprig.

Lemon Soda: Spoon 2 to 3 tablespoons Lemonade Syrup into a tall ice-filled glass. Fill the remainder of the glass with club soda or cola. Decorate with a lemon slice.

Wine Cooler: Add 2 to 3 tablespoons Lemonade Syrup to 1/4 cup sparkling rosé wine. Pour into a tall ice-filled glass. Fill remainder of glass with club soda. Stir. Decorate with a lemon slice.

Hot Spiced Lemonade

A perfect drink for a cold winter's eve.

7 cinnamon sticks
1/4 teaspoon whole cloves
1/4 teaspoon whole allspice
2-1/2 cups water
1-1/4 cups Lemonade Syrup (see opposite page)

In a small saucepan over low heat, simmer 1 of the cinnamon sticks, the cloves and allspice in water 10 minutes. Strain and discard spices. Add Lemonade Syrup. Heat 1 minute. Pour into punch cups or small teacups. Decorate with remaining cinnamon sticks. Makes 6 servings.

⊰⊙⊱

Lemon Ice Punch

Very refreshing and easy to prepare.

1 quart Lemon Sorbet (page 108)
4 cups (32 oz.) chilled apple juice
4 cups (32 oz.) chilled white grape juice
4 cups (32 oz.) chilled club soda
Maraschino cherries
Mint sprigs (optional)

Prepare Lemon Sorbet. Combine apple juice, grape juice and club soda in a punch bowl. Float Lemon Sorbet, cherries and mint sprigs, if using, in punch. Makes 16 to 20 servings.

Sparkling Lemon Punch

*A lemon punch with a true kick. There's no need
to wonder why they keep returning to the punch bowl.*

1 cup Lemonade Syrup (page 112)
8 cups (64 oz.) chilled apple juice
8 cups (64 oz.) chilled pineapple juice
4 cups (32 oz.) chilled sparkling Burgundy wine or
   rosé wine
8 cups (64 oz.) chilled club soda
Ice cubes
Lemon slices
Strawberries
Pineapple chunks

In a large punch bowl, combine Lemonade Syrup, apple juice, pineapple juice, wine, club soda and ice cubes. Float lemon slices, strawberries and pineapple chunks on top. Makes 32 to 40 servings.

Metric Conversion Chart

Comparison to Metric Measure				
When You Know	**Symbol**	**Multiply By**	**To Find**	**Symbol**
teaspoons	tsp	5.0	milliliters	ml
tablespoons	tbsp	15.0	milliliters	ml
fluid ounces	fl. oz.	30.0	milliliters	ml
cups	c	0.24	liters	l
pints	pt.	0.47	liters	l
quarts	qt.	0.95	liters	l
ounces	oz.	28.0	grams	g
pounds	lb.	0.45	kilograms	kg
Fahrenheit	F	5/9 (after subtracting 32)	Celsius	C

Liquid Measure to Milliliters

1/4 teaspoon	=	1.25 milliliters
1/2 teaspoon	=	2.5 milliliters
3/4 teaspoon	=	3.75 milliliters
1 teaspoon	=	5.0 milliliters
1-1/4 teaspoons	=	6.25 milliliters
1-1/2 teaspoons	=	7.5 milliliters
1-3/4 teaspoons	=	8.75 milliliters
2 teaspoons	=	10.0 milliliters
1 tablespoon	=	15.0 milliliters
2 tablespoons	=	30.0 milliliters

Fahrenheit to Celsius

F	C
200—205	95
220—225	105
245—250	120
275	135
300—305	150
325—330	165
345—350	175
370—375	190
400—405	205
425—430	220
445—450	230
470—475	245
500	260

Liquid Measure to Liters

1/4 cup	=	0.06 liters
1/2 cup	=	0.12 liters
3/4 cup	=	0.18 liters
1 cup	=	0.24 liters
1-1/4 cups	=	0.3 liters
1-1/2 cups	=	0.36 liters
2 cups	=	0.48 liters
2-1/2 cups	=	0.6 liters
3 cups	=	0.72 liters
3-1/2 cups	=	0.84 liters
4 cups	=	0.96 liters
4-1/2 cups	=	1.08 liters
5 cups	=	1.2 liters
5-1/2 cups	=	1.32 liters

Index